Janelle Ho and
Helen Pearson

Australian Curriculum Edition

Name: ______________________________

Class: ______________________________

Contents

SLLURP

SLLURP summarises the spelling strategies that you can use to learn new words.

Say	Say the word carefully and slowly to yourself.
Listen	Listen to how each part of the word sounds in sequence.
Look	Look at the patterns of letters in the word and the shape of the word.
Understand	Understand rules, word meanings and word origins.
Remember	Remember all the similar words you can already spell and relate this knowledge to any new word.
Practise	Practise writing the word until it is firmly fixed in your long-term memory.

Spelling Rules! Student Book 1 (ISBN 9780655092674) © Janelle Ho, Helen Pearson

Scope and Sequence

UNIT	SKILL FOCUS				OTHER	WORD LIST
	Vowels	Consonants	Letter patterns	Rules and tips		
1	short sounds	digraphs			than/then	rip, dish, quit, quick, ban, than, shack, let, moth, luck
2	ee, short oo					see, bee, feet, week, sheep, look, book, foot, good, wool
3		ll		suffix ed		all, wall, fall, fell, shall, dull, full, pull, walk, talk
4		st				stop, step, still, stick, rest, fast, list, lost, must, last
5		sl, sm				slip, slop, slap, slug, slid, sly, asleep, small, smell, smash
6	REVISION					
7			er		family words	mother, father, brother, sister, elder, taller, smaller, faster, baby, family
8		short y as vowel sound		suffix y		jelly, silly, hilly, happy, pretty, sunny, hurry, sleepy, hobby, body
9	a-e, e-e					ate, cake, take, late, date, name, awake, here, eve, these
10	i-e, o-e, u-e					like, hide, smile, fine, toe, nose, hope, stone, rude, ruler
11		ch		irregular plurals		chop, chat, chips, cheek, child, children, chase, rich, much, such
12	REVISION					
13		sk, sn, sp				spine, speech, snap, snore, snack, skin, skate, wasp, ask, desk
14		cl, fl, pl, bl				fly, flag, flash, clap, club, clock, plant, place, blast, blue
15	long oo					zoo, pool, room, moon, roof, tooth, food, spoon, school, balloon
16		final s, ss, zz; soft c		ss and zz don't start a word		kiss, mess, fuss, class, dress, plus, minus, cents, recess, buzz
17		nd				end, send, sand, kind, wind, pond, stand, handshake, grandmother, grandfather
18	REVISION					
19		br, cr, dr, gr, pr, tr			of/off	tree, crab, frog, from, pram, drive, grape, green, broom, friend
20		nt				ant, want, went, sent, spent, bent, front, hunt, aunt, uncle
21	ou					our, loud, cloud, house, mouse, shout, mouth, found, around, about
22			ow			owl, mow, how, slow, show, grow, down, down, brown, allow, yellow
23		ng		suffix ing		hang, sang, king, bring, thing, song, belong, hung, sting, swing
24	REVISION					
25		nk				ink, pink, wink, stink, think, drink, bank, thank, drank, skunk
26	ea				be/bee, sea/see, bean/been, meat/meet, weak/week	eat, ear, sea, meat, cheat, leaf, near, each, teacher, clean
27			ar			arm, car, park, dark, star, start, hard, barn, smart, farmer
28			ay, oy		to/two/too, by/buy	say, play, stay, tray, today, away, boy, enjoy, toy, buy
29			ir, or			bird, girl, stir, dirty, shirt, fork, torn, short, sport, cord
30	REVISION					
31					one/won, two/too, four/for, eight/ate	one, two, three, four, five, six, seven, eight, nine, ten
32			ld	comparative suffix er	silent t	old, cold, gold, told, sold, hold, held, bald, build, world
33	ai		air		stare/stair, sail/sale	air, hair, chair, stair, tail, sail, snail, train, wait, said
34		wh				who, why, when, where, what, which, whose, wheel, white, wheat
35	REVISION					

Note to Teachers and Parents

Spelling Rules!

Some students are natural spellers. But the vast majority of students need formal, systematic and sequential instruction about the way spelling works and the strategies they can use to become independent, confident spellers and spelling risk-takers.

The *Spelling Rules!* program is based on sound linguistic and pedagogical theory. It is informed by research into how students of different ages acquire and apply spelling skills, and how those skills move from the working to the long-term memory. The program closely follows the Australian English curriculum. *Australian Curriculum: English* references are provided in the Teacher Resource Books. The program consists of seven student books, fully supported by two Teacher Resource Books.

Each student book contains units of work, with each unit designed to be used over the course of a week. The content of each unit simultaneously develops new skills and reinforces skills from previous units. The introduction of new sounds and letter patterns is logically sequenced and takes into account both frequency of use and complexity. Where appropriate, topic words from other curriculum areas such as mathematics, science and social sciences are included. When spelling rules are introduced, only known sounds and letter patterns are used so that students focus on one skill at a time. Regular revision units enable teachers to assess student progress and reinforce key rules and patterns from previous units.

The *Spelling Rules!* program also incorporates elements of self-assessment. A simple reflection activity allows students to assess their own progress and provides you with a starting point for discussion.

Spelling knowledge

Learning to spell involves developing different kinds of spelling knowledge:

- **Kinaesthetic knowledge** – the physical feeling when saying different sounds and words, and when writing the shapes of letters and words
- **Phonological knowledge** – how a word sounds and the patterns of sounds in words
- **Visual knowledge** – how letters and words look and the visual patterns in words
- **Morphemic knowledge** – the meaning or function of words or parts of words
- **Etymological knowledge** – the origins and history of words and the effect this has on spelling patterns.

Icons used in Student Book 1

The following icons identify the main spelling strategy that students will use to complete an activity.

Say the word. (Kinaesthetic knowledge) These activities ask students to experience how sounds feel in the mouth and jaw. Changing the positions of the jaw, lips, and tongue changes the sounds we make. Encourage students to pronounce the sounds and words accurately. If they mispronounce a sound or word, they may misrepresent it in writing.

Listen to the word. (Phonological knowledge) These activities focus on discriminating between different sounds and breaking up words into syllables or individual sound segments (phonemes).

Look at the word. (Visual knowledge) These activities help students to see how the sound is represented using combinations of letters, and to associate this visual pattern with what they are hearing. Students will develop the ability to know when a word does or does not 'look right'.

Understand the word. (Morphemic and etymological knowledge) These activities focus on word meanings, word families, prefixes and suffixes, spelling rules, word origins and so on – all of which help embed spelling in the long-term memory.

Practise writing the word. (Kinaesthetic knowledge) These activities develop students' awareness of the physical movement involved in writing the word. By practising writing the word a number of times and in different contexts, the spelling becomes embedded in the long-term memory.

This icon highlights useful spelling rules.

This icon tells students that a special clue or hint is provided for an activity. It may be a spelling, grammar or punctuation convention, or a definition of a useful term.

Encourages students to assess their progress through each unit.

Spelling Rules! Student Book 1 (ISBN 9780655092674) © Janelle Ho, Helen Pearson

Student Book 1

Units of work

Student Book 1 contains 35 weekly units of work. See the **Scope and Sequence** chart on page 3 for more information. Each revision unit gives students an opportunity to self-assess. A simple reflection activity allows students to judge their personal progress and provides you with a starting point for discussion.

Word lists

In *Student Book 1*, each unit (except Revision) has a list of ten spelling words. The core words in the lists have been chosen to support the learning focus and strategies being taught in the unit.

Spelling lists enable a spelling element to be focused on, and there are sufficient examples to consolidate the teaching point. Topic words come from other curriculum areas, such as mathematics and social sciences. In addition, homophones and words that are easily confused with each other are explained and practised.

SLLURP

Each word list begins with a reminder for students to SLLURP. SLLURP summarises the strategies that will help spelling move from students' working memory to their long-term memory. These strategies are provided on page 2, for easy reference.

Unit at a glance

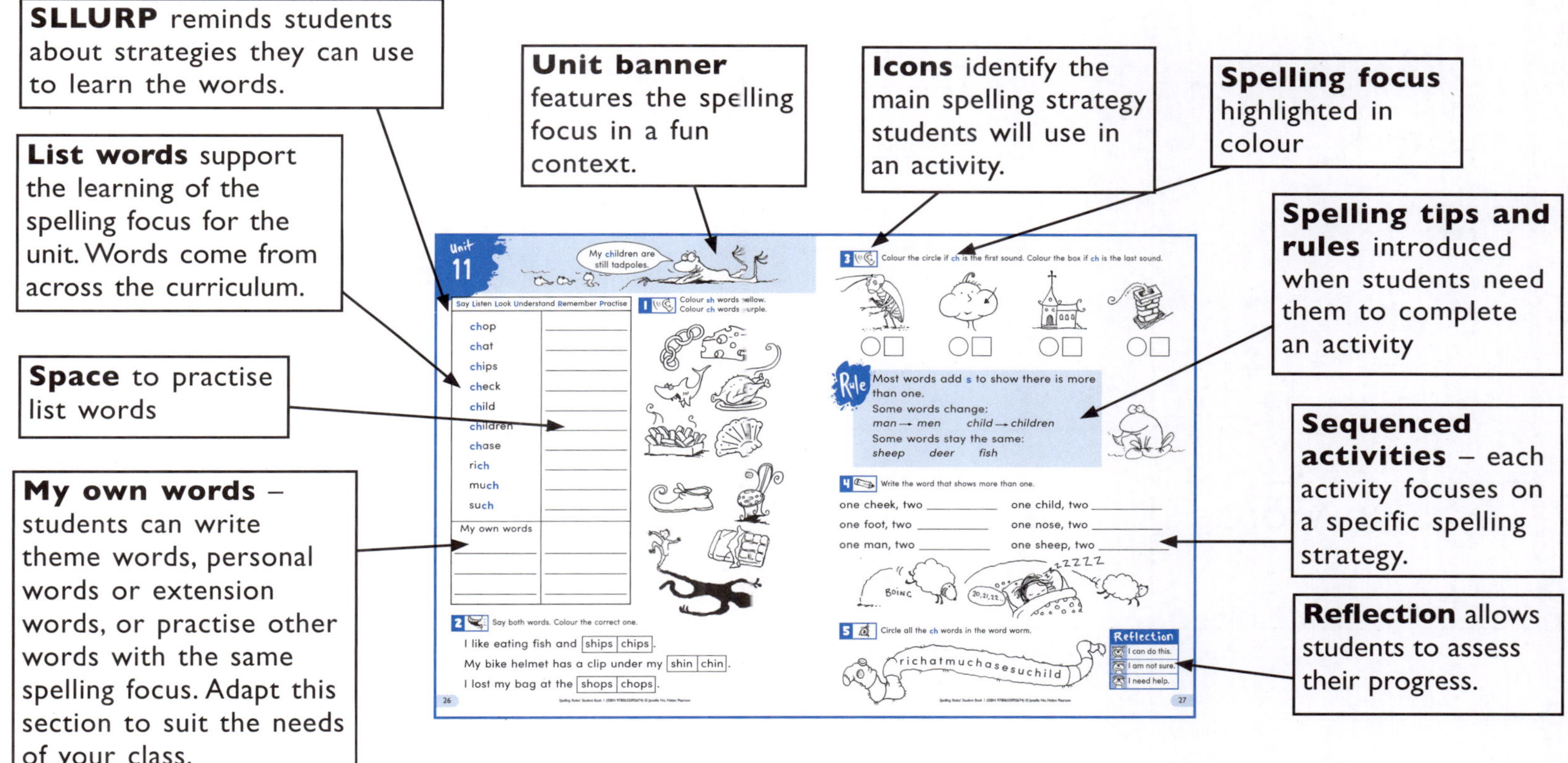

Spelling Rules! Teacher Resource Book F–2

Full teacher support for *Student Book 1* is provided by *Spelling Rules! Teacher Resource Book F–2*. Here you will find valuable background information about spelling development and spelling knowledge, along with practical resources, such as:

- teaching tips for every unit in *Student Book 1*
- extra word lists
- strategies for teaching spelling
- guidelines for assessing spelling and diagnosing spelling errors
- activities to support struggling spellers
- worthwhile extension for more able spellers.

Unit 1

Say Listen Look Understand Remember Practise	
rip	______
dish	______
quit	______
quick	______
ban	______
than	______
shack	______
let	______
moth	______
luck	______
My own words	
______	______
______	______
______	______

1 Write a list word that rhymes.

fish ______

ran ______

pack ______

buck ______

wet ______

2 Look at each word. Write the list word that is inside it.

trip ______

toilet ______

band ______

mother ______

quite ______

3 Write **a**, **e**, **i**, **o** or **u**.

n__ck

t__ck

d__ck

s__ck

s__ck

Spelling Rules! Student Book 1 (ISBN 9780655092674) © Janelle Ho, Helen Pearson

Say each word. Draw a line between each sound. The first one has been done.

b/a/n	rip	luck	quit
moth	than	dish	shack

Write the words.

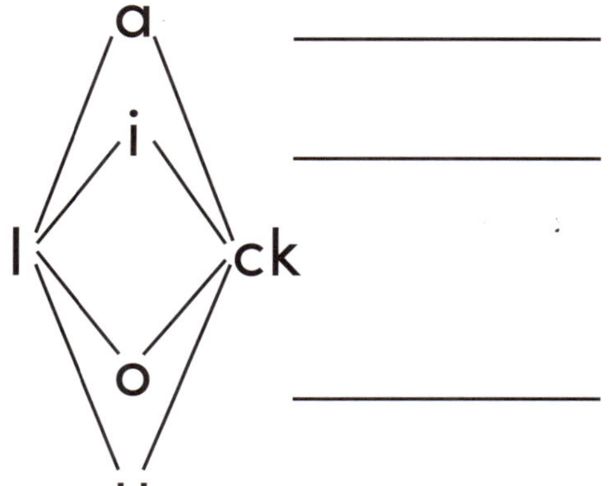

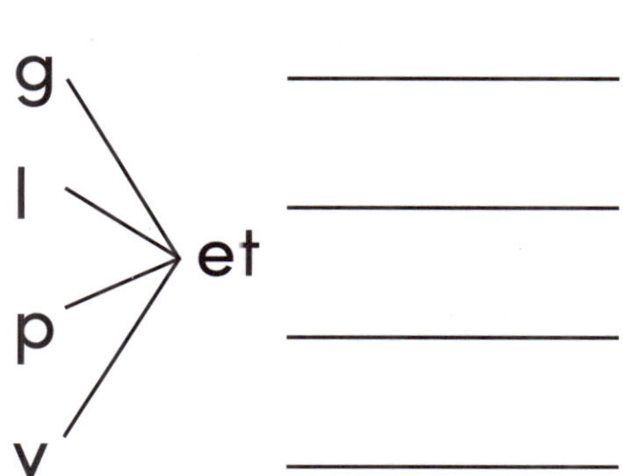

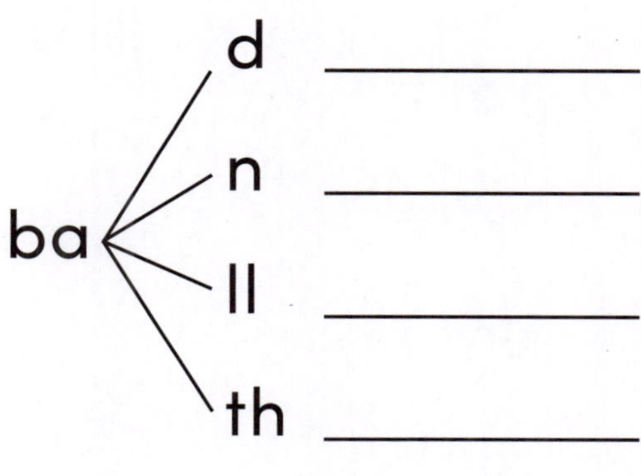

Say both words. Colour the correct one.

Ducks | quack | quick | when they want food.

Shut your eyes and make a | wash | wish |.

The | moth | both | flew at me and gave me a | shock | shot |.

than shows a comparison. **then** shows the next event.

Write the correct word.

I am shyer ____________ my sister.

I hit the ball and ____________ I ran!

Unit 2

Ouch!
The book fell
on my foot.

Say Listen Look Understand Remember Practise	
see	______
bee	______
feet	______
week	______
sheep	______
look	______
book	______
foot	______
good	______
wool	______
My own words	
______	______
______	______
______	______

1 Write ee or oo to make the correct word.

h__ __k

w__ __l

qu__ __n

c__ __k

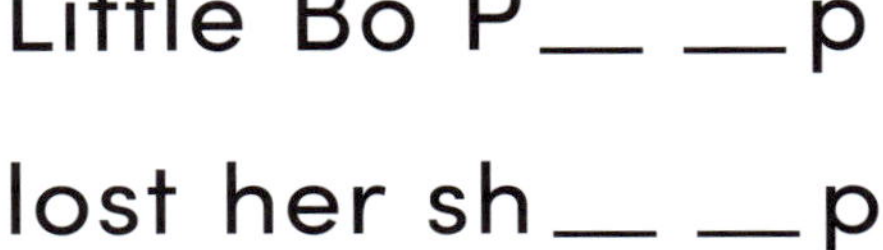

Little Bo P__ __p
lost her sh__ __p.
Where can she l__ __k?

I s__ __ a b__ __
on my f__ __t.

2 Use the letters to make ook words. Write the word again.

__ook ______ __ook ______

__ook ______ __ __ook ______

Spelling Rules! Student Book 1 (ISBN 9780655092674) © Janelle Ho, Helen Pearson

3 Write **ee** or **oo** to make list words.

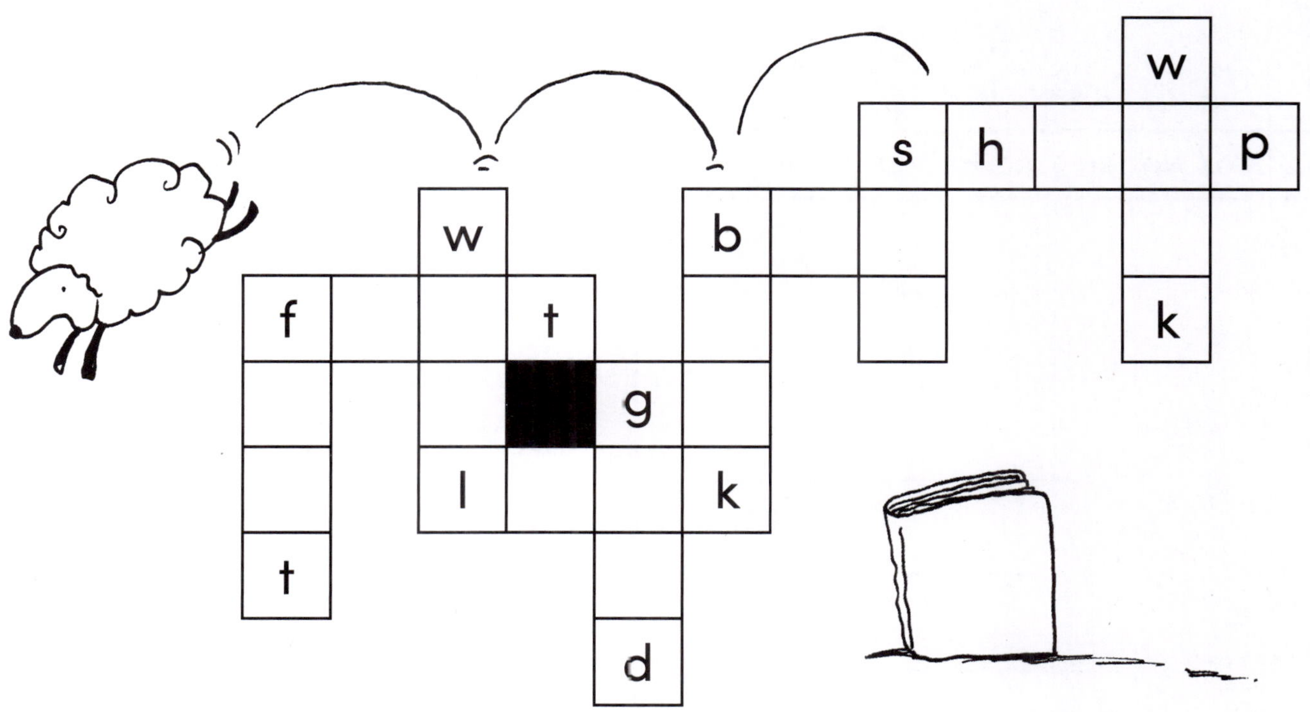

4 Change one letter to make a new word. Use the new word in a sentence.

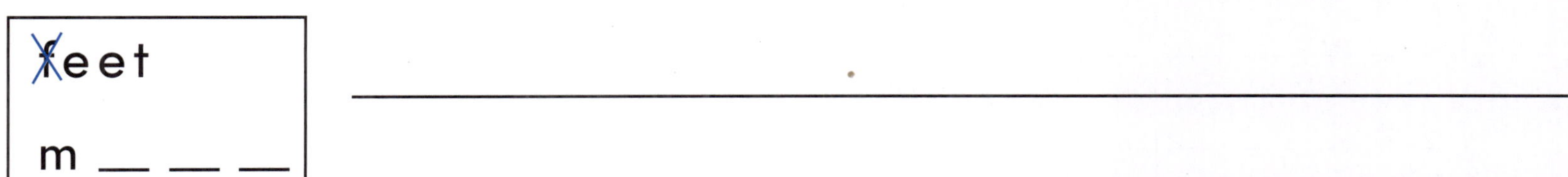

wood __ __ __ l	______________________________ ______________________________
hook t __ __ __	______________________________ ______________________________
feet m __ __ __	______________________________ ______________________________

5 Look for **ee** words in the word worm. Colour each **ee** word green.

Unit 3

Say Listen Look Understand Remember Practise	
all	
wall	
fall	
fell	
shall	
dull	
full	
pull	
walk	
talk	
My own words	

1 Write list words.

 sat on a ________.

 had a great ________.

All the king's horses

and ______ the king's men

could not put 

together again!

2 Say both words. Colour the correct one.

Kick the | bull | ball | to me.

| Pull | Pill | up your socks.

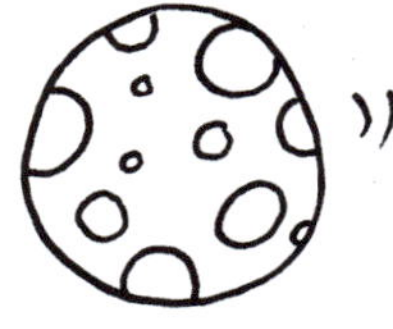

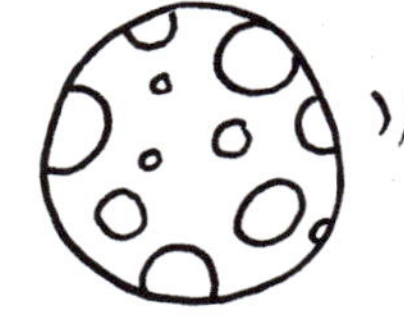

3 Use the words to make a wall.

a, all, ball

I, ill, fill

a, all, tall

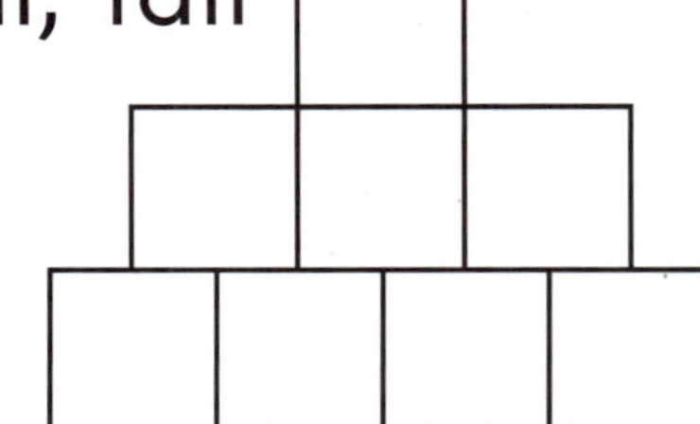

Spelling Rules! Student Book 1 (ISBN 9780655092674) © Janelle Ho, Helen Pearson

4 Vowels can make different sounds. Sort the words by listening to their sound.

ant	walk	call	lap
gull	dug	full	bull
shall	dull	hall	wool

a as in cat

____

____

____

a as in ball

____

____

____

u as in cup

____

____

____

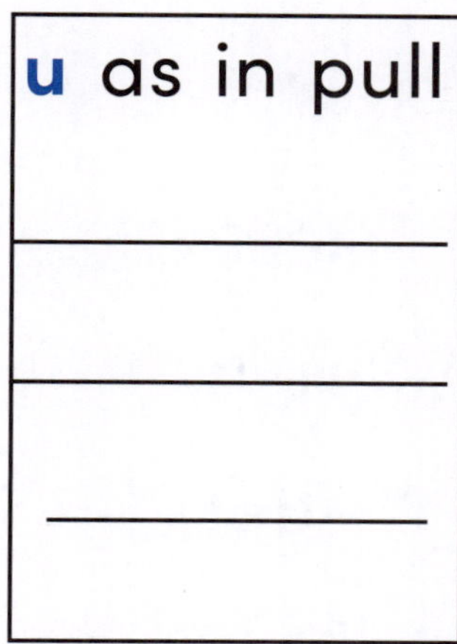

u as in pull

____

____

____

Some words add **ed** to show an action that happened in the past. *pack* ⟶ *packed*

5 Add **ed**.

look____ fill____ walk____

6 Colour the correct word.

I woke up when a bird | calls | called | loudly.

He | talks | talked | so slowly that we all felt sleepy.

Bill | packs | packed | his bag before he went to bed.

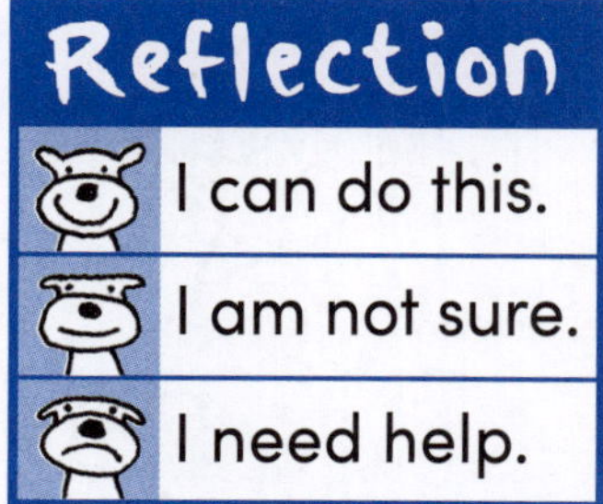

Unit 4

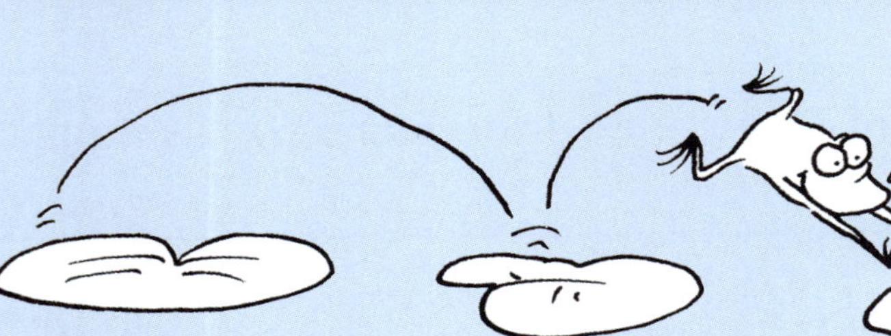

Say Listen Look Understand Remember Practise

stop	______
step	______
still	______
stick	______
rest	______
fast	______
list	______
lost	______
must	______
last	______
My own words	
______	______
______	______
______	______

1 Write list words.

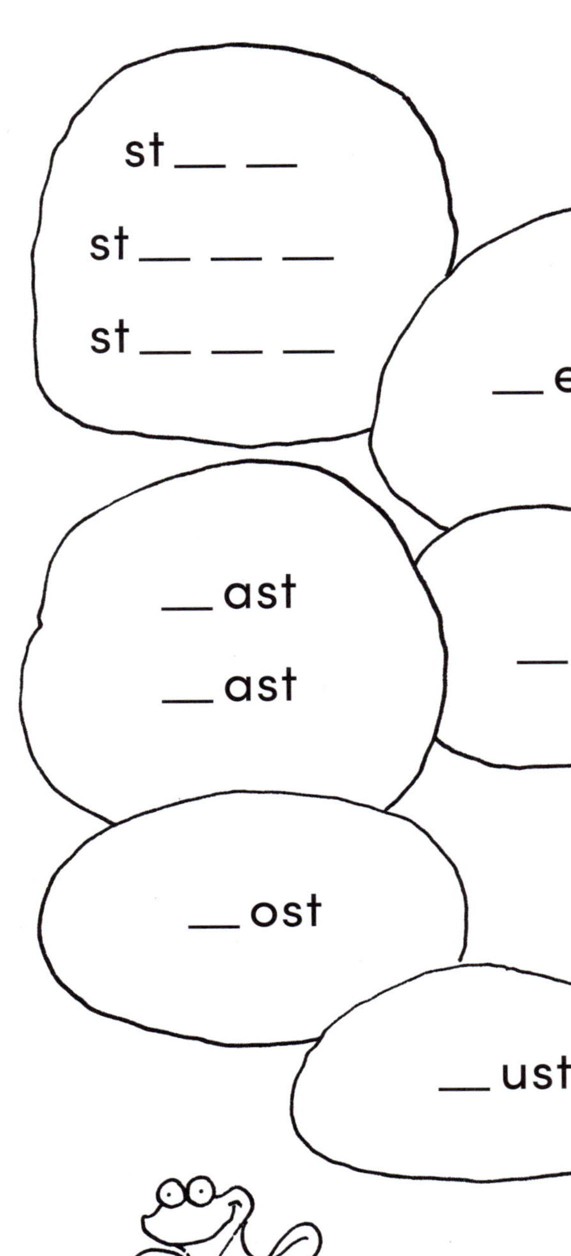

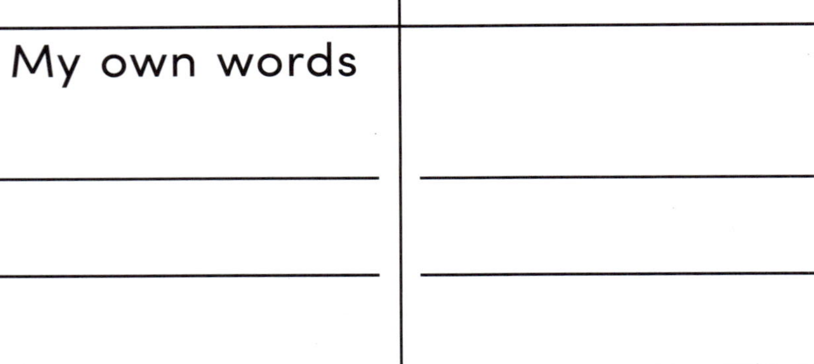

2 Colour the box if the word starts with **st**. Colour the circle if the word ends with **st**.

☐ ○ ☐ ○ ☐ ○ ☐ ○

Spelling Rules! Student Book 1 (ISBN 9780655092674) © Janelle Ho, Helen Pearson

3 Write a, e, i, o or u to make an st word on each step.

 Look for a small word in the list word. Write the small word.

stop ____________ must ____________

list ____________ last ____________

 Write a list word for each clue.

small branch ____________

take a nap ____________

not slow ____________

not first ____________ not moving ____________

 Write list words.

I play with my ____________ friend every day.

Have you seen my bag? I ____________ it.

____________ and look before you cross the street.

Don't ____________ in the mud.

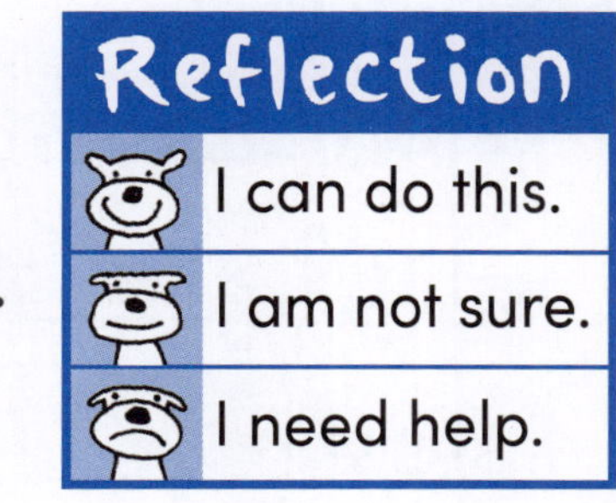

Unit 5

Slap on a hat when the sun is hot!

Say Listen Look Understand Remember Practise

slip	____________
slop	____________
slap	____________
slug	____________
slid	____________
sly	____________
asleep	____________
small	____________
smell	____________
smash	____________
My own words	
____________	____________
____________	____________
____________	____________

1 Write list words.

____________ on a T-shirt,

____________ on sunscreen,

____________ on a hat

before you go out in the sun!

Don't fall ____________ in the sun.

Something is cooking. What can you ____________?

2 Change the underlined letter to make a list word.

slam ____________

slot ____________

slash ____________

spy ____________

sled ____________

stall ____________

Spelling Rules! Student Book 1 (ISBN 9780655092674) © Janelle Ho, Helen Pearson

Listen to the beginning of each word.
Write **sl** or **sm** in the box.

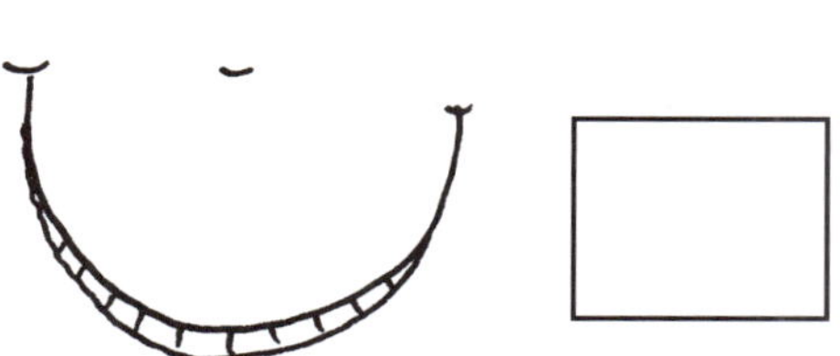 ☐  ☐  ☐

Rearrange the letters to make list words.

lips ____________

lids ____________

laps ____________

Rearrange the letters to make a word.

lmsal ________________

wlak ________________

cqiku ________________

Say both words. Colour the correct word.

I like the | small | smell | of popcorn.

Our baby fell | asleep | sleep | on my lap.

Try not to | slip | slid | on the step.

| Slogs | Slugs | must stay out of the sun.

Write a sentence about each picture.

____

____

____

____

Reflection

| I can do this. |
| I am not sure. |
| I need help. |

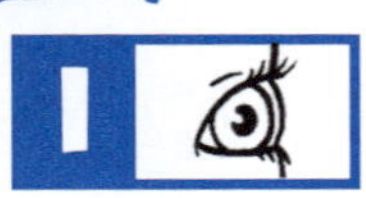

1 Colour the words.

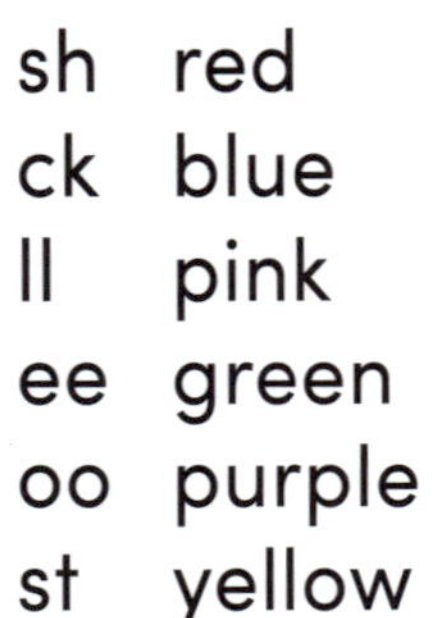

sh	red
ck	blue
ll	pink
ee	green
oo	purple
st	yellow

Which word is not coloured? ________________

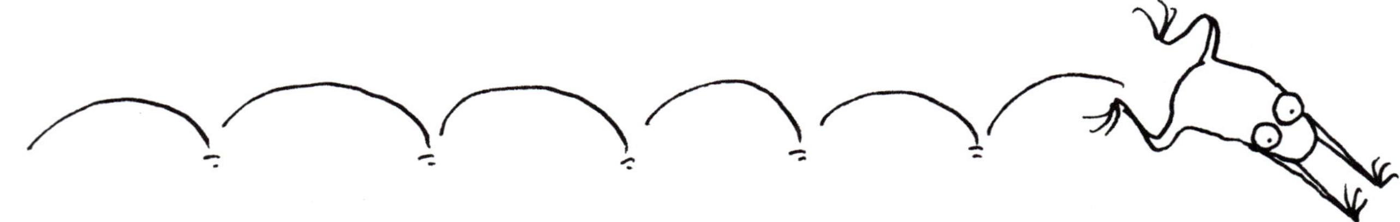

2 Change one letter in each word to make a new word.

shop	wish	lick	bell
________	________	________	________
stop	list	slop	smell
________	________	________	________
see	hood		
________	________		

Spelling Rules! Student Book 1 (ISBN 9780655092674) © Janelle Ho, Helen Pearson

Two words can join together to make a new word.

sun + hat ⟶ sunhat

3 Join the two words to make a new word. Draw a picture to match.

back + pack

____

week + end

____

foot + ball

____

foot + path

____

4 Label the picture. Use the words in the wall.

slug wool foot wall

bull step bee boot

nest hoof sheep book

Spelling Rules! Student Book 1 (ISBN 9780655092674)

Unit 7

Say Listen Look Understand Remember Practise	
mother	____________
father	____________
brother	____________
sister	____________
elder	____________
taller	____________
smaller	____________
faster	____________
baby	____________
family	____________
My own words	
____________	____________
____________	____________
____________	____________

1 Look at each family. Fill in the missing words.

Kim Helen Nick Tim Sam

Helen is Sam's ____________.

Nick is his ____________.

Tim is his ____________.

Kim is his ____________.

Helen will have a ____________ soon.

Then there will be six people in Sam's ____________.

Ling Lee

Lee has no br________ or si________.

Ling is her ____________.

Tareq Reem Yusef

____________ is Yusef's ____________.

____________ is his ____________.

Spelling Rules! Student Book 1 (ISBN 9780655092674) © Janelle Ho, Helen Pearson

 What is my family doing? Write words that end in **er**.

I am sitting on the step.

My ____________ sits at the computer.

My ____________ cooks lunch.

My ____________ reads a book.

My ____________ is fast asleep.

I will see my grandmother tomorrow. She is an ______________ and will teach me how to care for Country.

A **syllable** makes one beat in a word.
A syllable has a vowel sound in it.

mum = 1 syllable *mother* = 2 syllables

grandmother = 3 syllables

 Say each word. How many syllables can you hear in each word? Write 1, 2 or 3.

 ◯  ◯  ◯  ◯ 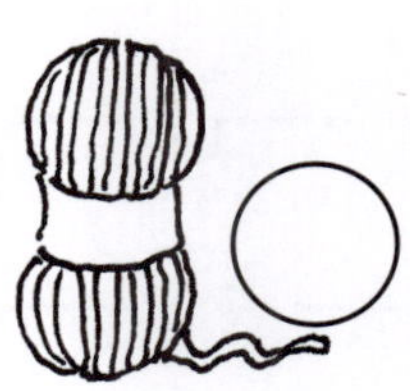 ◯ 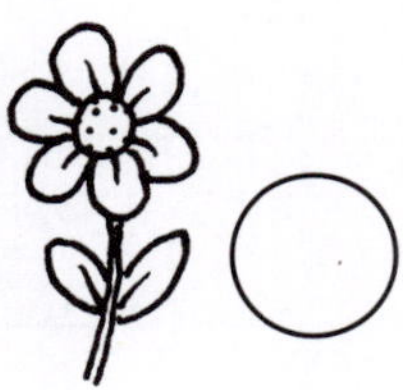 ◯

 Add the ending to the word. Write the new word.

small + er ____________ quick + er ____________

What does the **er** ending do?

____

Reflection

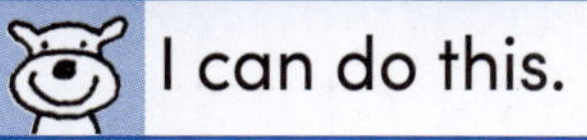 I can do this.

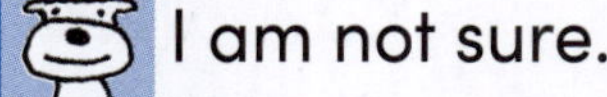 I am not sure.

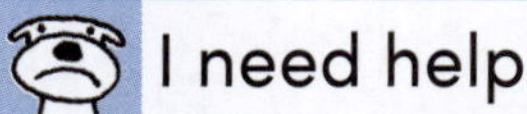 I need help.

Unit 8

Say Listen Look Understand Remember Practise	
jelly	______
silly	______
hilly	______
happy	______
pretty	______
sunny	______
hurry	______
sleepy	______
hobby	______
body	______
My own words	
______	______
______	______
______	______

1  Fill in double letters. Most of the words are list words.

This je__ __y is very wo__ __ly.

We all like fu__ __y books.

It will be su__ __y this weekend.

Jonny has a si __ __ y hat on.

Let's all try to be ha__ __y today.

I have to hu __ __ y to school.

The doll has a pre__ __y dress.

Penny lives on a hi__ __y str__ __t.

2  Colour the box if **y** has a short sound as in **mummy** or **daddy**.

cry
very
body

they
dry
sleepy

shy
dusty
sticky

Spelling Rules! Student Book 1 (ISBN 9780655092674) © Janelle Ho, Helen Pearson

Fill in **a**, **o** or **u** and **y**.

d__dd__   l__ll__   s__nn__   w__bbl__

h__pp__   h__bb__   h__rr__   sl__pp__

Some words add **y** to make a describing word.

sleep → sleepy

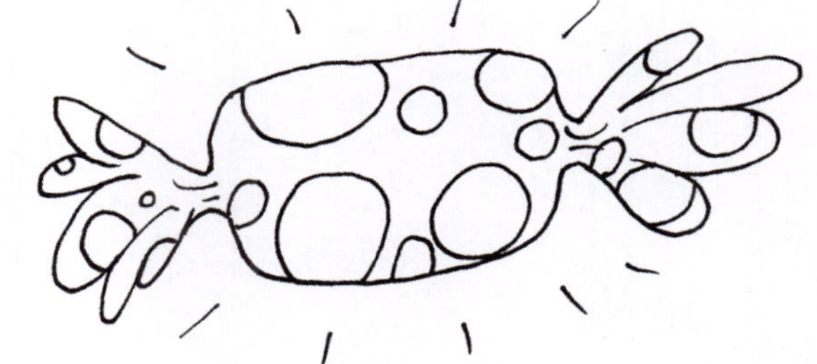

Add **y** to make new words.

rust __________   dirt __________   dust __________

luck __________   mess __________   smell __________

rock __________   cheek __________   hill __________

Write these sentences again with a space between each word.

Mypuppyisverymuddy. ____________________

Isyourtoothwobbly? ____________________

Redjellyissoyummy. ____________________

Read each word. Cross out the word that doesn't belong.

skinny	slim	sticky	thin
shy	muddy	grubby	dusty
funny	jolly	body	witty

Reflection

 I can do this.

 I am not sure.

I need help.

Unit 9

Say Listen Look Understand Remember Practise	
ate	______________
cake	______________
take	______________
late	______________
date	______________
name	______________
awake	______________
here	______________
eve	______________
these	______________
My own words	
______________	______________
______________	______________
______________	______________

1 Circle the picture if you hear a long **a** sound.

2 Say both words. Colour the correct one.

I saw a lion | at | ate | the zoo.

I left my book | her | here |.

Don't walk on the | mat | mate | with muddy shoes.

Use the letters in the word machine to make words.

___________ ___________

___________ ___________

___________ ___________

___________ ___________

____

Write list words.

Kate is eating chocolate __________.

__________ are my favourite shoes.

I stayed __________ for the New Year's ________ fireworks last year.

Write a plural word.

Chocolate, carrot, fruit and mud are all ______________.

Ali, Li Ling, Nazim and David are all ______________.

Tennis, football and cricket are all ______________.

Poodles, greyhounds and pugs are all ______________.

6 Circle all the **a–e** words in the word worm.

Reflection

I can do this.

I am not sure.

I need help.

Unit 10

Spelling

More Spelling

Even More Spelling

I like to play hide-and-seek!

Say Listen Look Understand Remember Practise	
like	____________
hide	____________
smile	____________
fine	____________
toe	____________
nose	____________
hope	____________
stone	____________
rude	____________
ruler	____________
My own words	
____________	____________
____________	____________
____________	____________

1  Write a list word that rhymes. Make another new word that also rhymes.

ride	____________	sl __ __ __
line	____________	sh __ __ __
hose	____________	r __ __ __
bone	____________	c __ __ __
spike	____________	b __ __ __
cope	____________	r __ __ __
Joe	____________	h __ __
tile	____________	f __ __ __

2 Add **e** to make a word with a different sound.

to	hop	not	kit
to __	hop __	not __	kit __

Spelling Rules! Student Book 1 (ISBN 9780655092674) © Janelle Ho, Helen Pearson

3 Write the missing vowels.

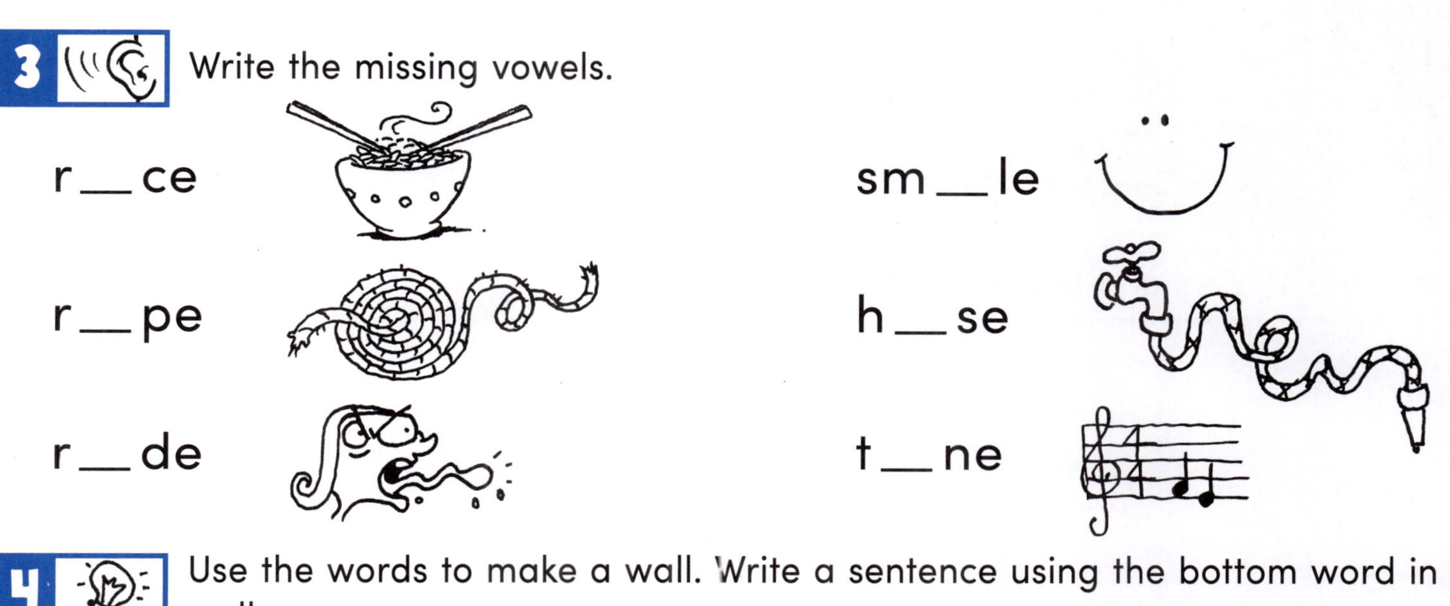

r__ce

r__pe

r__de

sm__le

h__se

t__ne

4 Use the words to make a wall. Write a sentence using the bottom word in each wall.

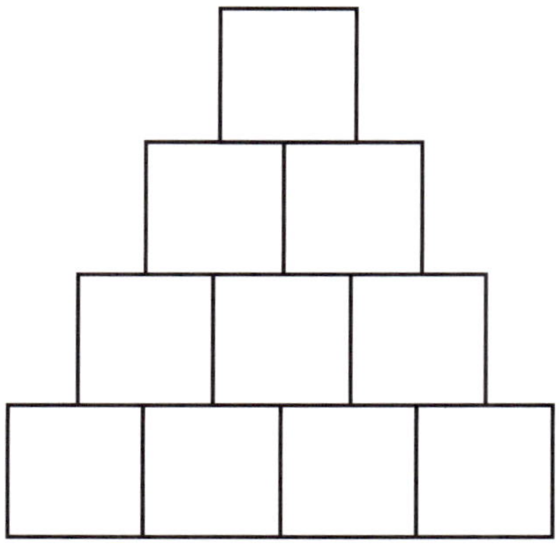

I, in, fin, fine

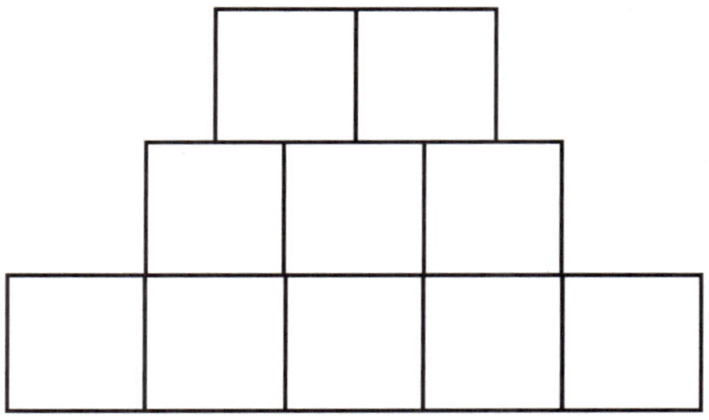

on, one, stone

5 Say both words. Colour the correct word.

I | hop | hope | I get a bike for my birthday.

Mike | hid | hide | his bag under his bed.

Do you | lick | like | playing computer games?

It is cold. I do | not | note | want to swim.

Unit 11

Say Listen Look Understand Remember Practise	
chop	____________
chat	____________
chips	____________
check	____________
child	____________
children	____________
chase	____________
rich	____________
much	____________
such	____________
My own words	
____________	____________
____________	____________
____________	____________

1 Colour **sh** words yellow.
Colour **ch** words purple.

2 Say both words. Colour the correct one.

I like eating fish and | ships | chips |.

My bike helmet has a clip under my | shin | chin |.

I lost my bag at the | shops | chops |.

Spelling Rules! Student Book 1 (ISBN 9780655092674) © Janelle Ho, Helen Pearson

 Colour the circle if **ch** is the first sound. Colour the box if **ch** is the last sound.

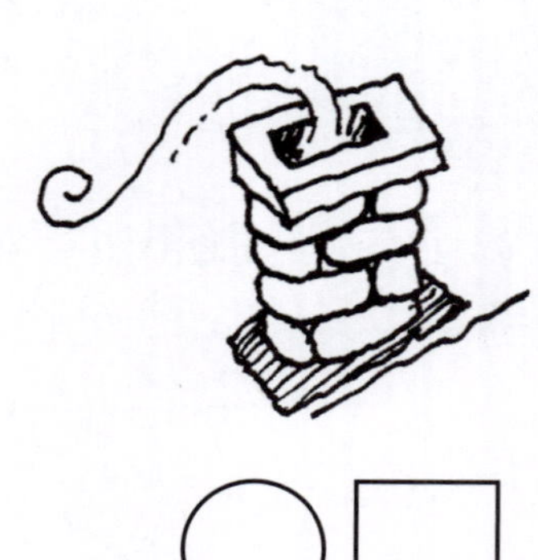

Most words add **s** to show there is more than one.

Some words change:

man → *men* *child* → *children*

Some words stay the same:

sheep *deer* *fish*

 Write the word that shows more than one.

one cheek, two ____________ one child, two ____________

one foot, two ____________ one nose, two ____________

one man, two ____________ one sheep, two ____________

 Circle all the **ch** words in the word worm.

Spelling Rules! Student Book 1 (ISBN 9780655092674) © Janelle Ho, Helen Pearson

Colour the fish with a short vowel sound orange.
Colour the fish with a long vowel sound yellow.

Add **s** or **ed** to make a correct sentence.

Nish blame____ me but I don't have his game.

Sally told me that she wish____ for a new backpack.

Grandma always fill____ my plate with yummy food.

After we cleared the shed, we rest____. Then we pull____ out the weeds in the garden.

Joe need____ his crayons today but he left them at home.

Write a word that is the opposite.

bad ____________	poor ____________
found ____________	first ____________
early ____________	asleep ____________
adult ____________	slow ____________

4 Make a word to match each clue.

l / t / s → ame

____________ not different

____________ horse with a sore foot

____________ not wild

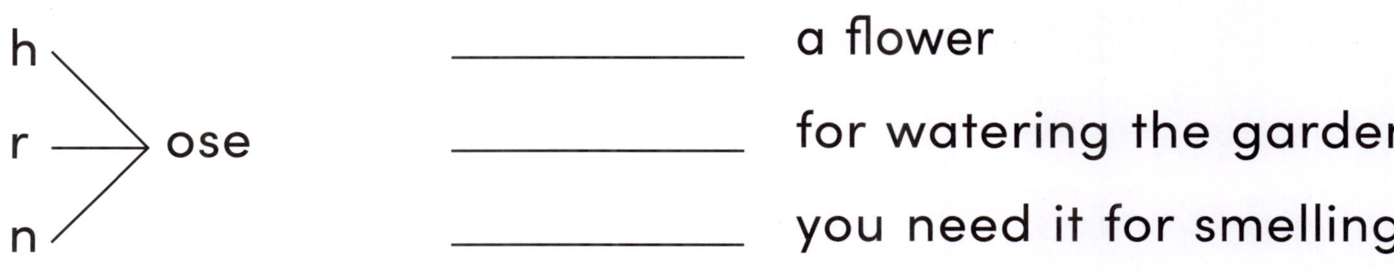

h / r / n → ose

____________ a flower

____________ for watering the garden

____________ you need it for smelling

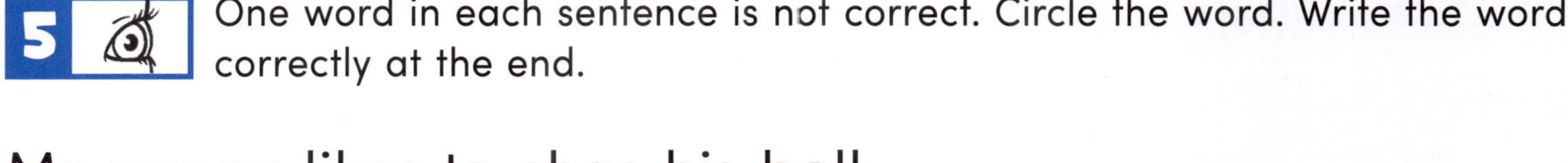

5 One word in each sentence is not correct. Circle the word. Write the word correctly at the end.

My puppy likes to chas his ball. ____________

Moths hide when it is suny. ____________

My bruther is taller than me. ____________

We were all sleppy by ten o'clock. ____________

Use a roler to check the size of the box. ____________

6 Write about your hobby.

____

____

____

____

Unit 13

Say Listen Look Understand Remember Practise	
spine	______
speech	______
snap	______
snore	______
snack	______
skin	______
skate	______
wasp	______
ask	______
desk	______
My own words	
______	______
______	______
______	______

1 Write **sp**, **sn** or **sk** to show the first sounds in the word.

__ __   __ __

__ __   __ __

__ __   __ __

__ __   __ __

Ah choo

__ __   __ __

2 Write list words.

sp	______ ______
______	sp

sn	______ ______ ______

sk	______ ______
______	sk

Spelling Rules! Student Book 1 (ISBN 9780655092674) © Janelle Ho, Helen Pearson

 Write a word for each clue.

 Say both words. Colour the correct word.

The wind makes the clothes | spin | spine | on the line.

If you are hungry, have a | snack | snake |.

My dog has a black | stop | spot | on his back.

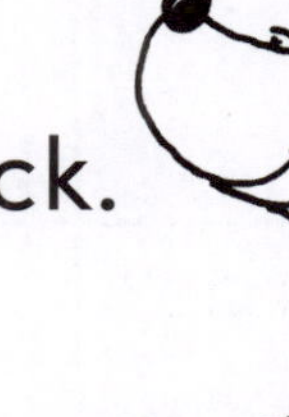

 Find a small word inside the big word. Write the small word.

task	skill	spine	wasp
________	________	________	________

6 Write words with **sk**, **sn** or **sp**.

I like to eat an apple as a _ _ _ _ _

after school. Today my apple had a black

_ _ _ _ on its red _ _ _ _.

Unit 14

Frogs can't **fl**y!

Say Listen Look Understand Remember Practise	
fly	________
flag	________
flash	________
clap	________
club	________
clock	________
plant	________
place	________
blast	________
blue	________
My own words	
________	________
________	________
________	________

1 Write **fl**, **cl** **pl** or **bl** to show the first sounds in the word.

__ __   __ __

__ __   __ __

__ __   __ __

__ __   __ __

Write a list word that rhymes.

sock	zoo	face	dash
________	________	________	________

3 Write the words. Match each word to its picture.

pl — um ____________

pl — ug ____________

pl — ant ____________

cl — ap ____________

cl — ip ____________

cl — ass ____________

sl — ug ____________

sl — ip ____________

sl — ide ____________

fl — ip ____________

fl — op ____________

4 Write the missing letters. Draw a picture for each sentence.

Eat everything on your

__ __ ate. Then you can go

and __ __ ay.

pl

The __ __ock strikes ten. The

children __ __ap and cheer.

cl

I need __ __ue __ __ocks to

make the sea.

bl

Unit 15

Say Listen Look Understand Remember Practise	
zoo	______
pool	______
room	______
moon	______
roof	______
tooth	______
food	______
spoon	______
school	______
balloon	______
My own words	
______	______
______	______
______	______

1 Write a list word in each shape.

2 Say the words. If **oo** makes the sound in t**oo**k, colour the picture red. If **oo** makes the sound in f**oo**d, colour the picture yellow.

Spelling Rules! Student Book 1 (ISBN 9780655092674) © Janelle Ho, Helen Pearson

When two words join together to make a new word, it is called a **compound** word.

Football is a compound word.

3 Write the names of these rooms. Write two more compound words of your own.

bed
bath → room
class

______
______
______

4 Proofread the story. There are six mistakes. Circle the mistakes. Write the words correctly at the end.

It is dark and cold. Dad and I sit on the roof to lock at the moon. I have warm botts on. We have food. It is cak and ice cream. Clang! I drop my spon. It falls off the roof and into the pooll. Splach! It is gone.

______ ______
______ ______
______ ______

Reflection

- I can do this.
- I am not sure.
- I need help.

Spelling Rules! Student Book 1 (ISBN 9780655092674) © Janelle Ho, Helen Pearson

Unit 16

I will not make a mess of my dress.

Say Listen Look Understand Remember Practise	
kiss	__________
mess	__________
fuss	__________
class	__________
dress	__________
plus	__________
minus	__________
cents	__________
recess	__________
buzz	__________
My own words	
__________	__________
__________	__________
__________	__________

1 Write list words.

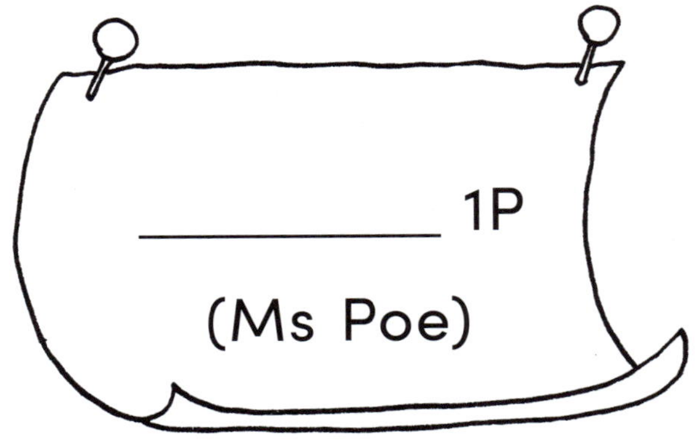

2 Write a list word that rhymes.

less	bus	miss	tents	fuzz
________	________	________	________	________

Spelling Rules! Student Book 1 (ISBN 9780655092674) © Janelle Ho, Helen Pearson

Say each word. Circle the words in which **c** makes a sound like **s**.

clap	rice	lunch	cent
face	recess	click	school

Write the list words.

Mum said, 'Sit still and don't __ __ __ __ !'

My sister sat in the mud. Her __ __ __ __ __ is dirty.

I need ten __ __ __ __ __ more to buy sushi at __ __ __ __ __ __ .

If one __ __ __ __ one is two, then two __ __ __ __ __ one is one.

ss and **zz** do not start a word.

Write **s**, **ss**, **z** or **zz**.

bu____

____oo

____orry

fi____

mi____

Reflection
I can do this.
I am not sure.
I need help.

Unit 17

Say Listen Look Understand Remember Practise	
end	
send	
sand	
kind	
wind	
pond	
stand	
handshake	
grandmother	
grandfather	
My own words	

1 Make words. Circle the word that sounds different.

b h l s w
and

______ ______

______ ______

______

2 Change one letter to make a list word.

bend ______ fond ______ and ______

wand ______ send ______ mind ______

Spelling Rules! Student Book 1 (ISBN 9780655092674) © Janelle Ho, Helen Pearson

A syllable makes one beat in a word. Say the underlined words. Write the number of syllables you hear.

My mother and I stand in the sand.

My grandmother holds my hand.

My grandfather stands in the water.

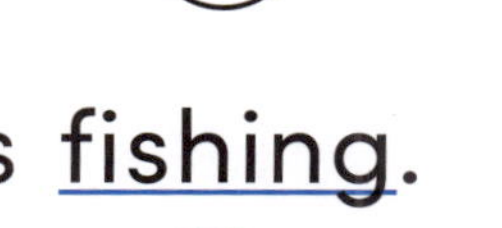

He is fishing.

Write the missing vowels.

Dad __nd I visited my gr__ndfather.

He lives __n a farm. He is k__nd.

The farm was cold. We saw the trees b__nd over because it was so w__ndy.

Make compound words.

hand + shake = ________________

hand + stand = ________________

grand + mother = ________________

grand + father = ________________

Colour the oval blue if **wind** rhymes with **kind**.
Colour the oval green if **wind** rhymes with **pinned**.

The (wind) blew dust in our eyes.

Try to (wind) the rope around the log.

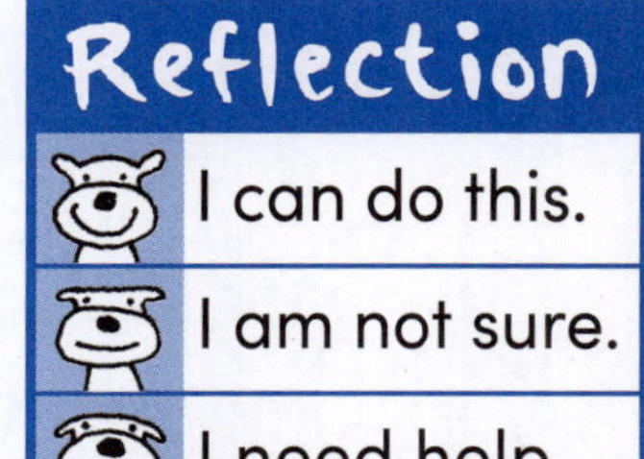

1 Use words from the box to complete the puzzles.

flap	roof	play	feet
room	flat	they	meet

blow in the wind

not hilly

not work

he and she

tool	eyes	book	spot
kiss	bike	snap	pool

a card game

a small mark

swim here

spade or rake

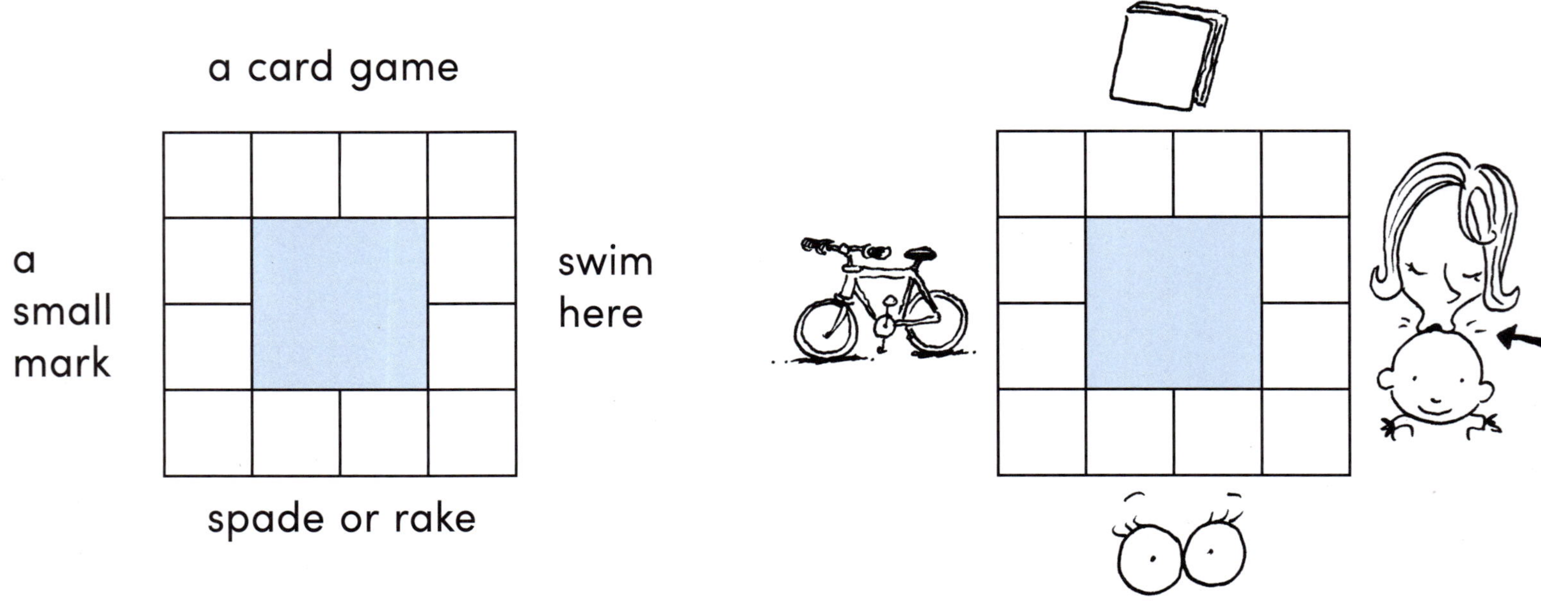

Spelling Rules! Student Book 1 (ISBN 9780655092674) © Janelle Ho, Helen Pearson

 Sometimes signs stand for words.

 A heart says love.

 A t__ __ __ says you are right.

 A cr__ __ __ says you are wrong.

 A pl__ __ sign says add together.

A mi__ __ __ sign says take away.

 Write the words in alphabetical order.

plug plate plus past pick

____

that then ten tap toss

____

 Proofread this story. There are six mistakes. Circle the mistakes. Write the words correctly at the end.

My brother Russ liks games. He is in the chess clubb at sckool. On Fridays, Russ sspends lunchtime in the classrom playing chess. He never winds!

__________ __________

__________ __________ __________ __________

Unit 19

I ate too many grapes.

Say Listen Look Understand Remember Practise	
tree	______
crab	______
frog	______
from	______
pram	______
drive	______
grape	______
green	______
broom	______
friend	______
My own words	
______	______
______	______
______	______

1 Write the first sound.

__ r   __ r

__ r   __ r

__ r   __ r

__ r   __ r

__ r   __ r

2 Change one letter to make a list word. Use the new word in a sentence.

~~g~~rab
c __ __ __

______
______
______

~~f~~ree
t __ __ __

______
______
______

Spelling Rules! Student Book 1 (ISBN 9780655092674) © Janelle Ho, Helen Pearson

3 Use the letters to make words.

gr

ab ub eet een ape and

_______________ _______________

_______________ _______________

_______________ _______________

tr

ee ap ip ack ot uck

_______________ _______________

_______________ _______________

_______________ _______________

4 Proofread this story. There are five mistakes. Circle the mistakes. Write the words correctly at the end.

Fran and I pretend we can drive. Fran likes to drive a train. I drive a tuck and use a brom to steer. Then I drip over a brik. I cut my toe. Mum told us to play on the grarss.

_______________ _______________ _______________

_______________ _______________

Tip Do not mix up **of** and **off**. *one* ***of*** *us* *turn it* ***off***

5 Write **of** or **off**.

Get _____ the bus at the last stop.

One _____ my eggs is still hot.

Reflection

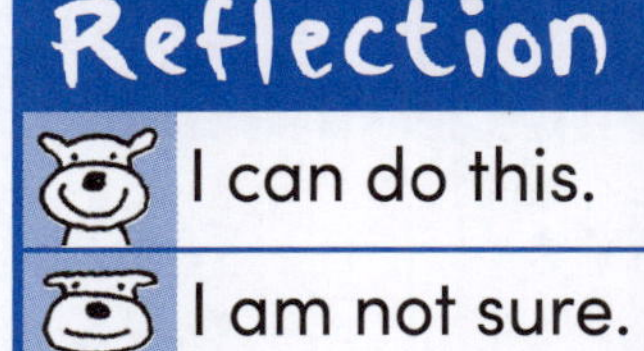

I can do this.

I am not sure.

I need help.

Unit 20

Say Listen Look Understand Remember Practise	
ant	________
want	________
went	________
sent	________
spent	________
bent	________
front	________
hunt	________
aunt	________
uncle	________
My own words	
________	________
________	________
________	________

1 Write the **nt** words in the tent. Write the **nd** words in the pond.

a, se, spe, b → nt

a, se, spe, b → nd

________ ________

________ ________

________ ________

________ ________

A sound can be shown using different letters.

2 Write the list words that have the same vowel sound.

hunt ________ ________

____

Spelling Rules! Student Book 1 (ISBN 9780655092674) © Janelle Ho, Helen Pearson

3 Read the story and fill in **nd** or **nt**.

I felt the wi__ __ a__ __ we__ __ to fi __ __ my kite. Aunt Min se__ __ it to me. She is ki__ __ and seems to know just what I wa__ __. Last year she gave me a te__ __ but I have be__ __ one of the poles. Dad needs to me__ __ it for me.

My dog Binty and I ran on the sa__ __. I watched my kite be__ __ and loop in the breeze. When it fell to la__ __ , we had to hu__ __ for it. Binty fou__ __ it. He began to bark a__ __ pa__ __. It was on the rocks with its tail waving like a long pla__ __.

Rule

Use **a** before a consonant.
Use **an** before a vowel.

4 Write **a** or **an**.

___ ant ___ tent ___ aunt ___ uncle

Tip

Most words add **ed** to show the past tense, but some verbs change. *is* → *was* *do* → *did*

5 Colour the correct word.

I | spend | spent | $3.00 on a pie. It was yummy.

Mum | send | sent | Aunty Lin a card when she was ill.

Ben and Jen | go | went | swimming every Sunday.

Reflection

I can do this.
I am not sure.
I need help.

Unit 21

CROAK!

Your croaking is very loud!

Say Listen Look Understand Remember Practise	
our	______
loud	______
cloud	______
house	______
mouse	______
shout	______
mouth	______
found	______
around	______
about	______
My own words	
______	______
______	______
______	______

1 Make **ou** words.

c, l, m, r, sh, s — ou — nt, th, r, t, d, nd

______

______

______

2 Write these words as two syllables.

about = ___ + ______

aloud = ___ + ______

around = ___ + ______

3 Arrange the words to make sentences. Add correct punctuation.

a found I mouse ______

live a in we house round ______

______

Spelling Rules! Student Book 1 (ISBN 9780655092674) © Janelle Ho, Helen Pearson

Cross out the word that does not rhyme.
Add a list word that rhymes.

loud	proud	sound	______________
mouth	mouse	blouse	______________

Write the **ou** words in the correct cloud.

south	out	ground	count
about	mount	mouth	round

nd

______________ ______________

th

______________ ______________

t

______________ ______________

nt

______________ ______________

6 Read the sentences and draw the picture.

Up in the sky I see a cloud that looks like a mouse. On the ground a man with a big mouth is shouting at a cat.

Unit 22

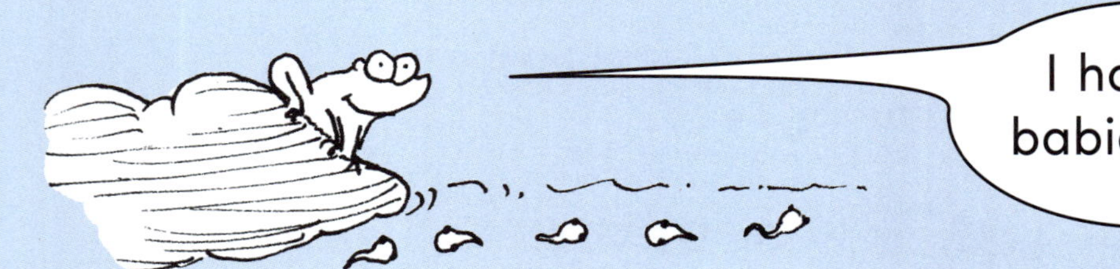

Say Listen Look Understand Remember Practise	
owl	______
mow	______
how	______
slow	______
show	______
grow	______
down	______
brown	______
allow	______
yellow	______
My own words	
______	______
______	______
______	______

1 Say each list word. Sort the words into the balloons.

ow makes the sound in brown

brown

______

______

______

______

ow makes the sound in yellow

yellow

______

______

______

______

2 Make compound words. Use a word from each box.

snow rain eye		man bow brow		______ ______ ______

Spelling Rules! Student Book 1 (ISBN 9780655092674) © Janelle Ho, Helen Pearson

Use the letters to make words.

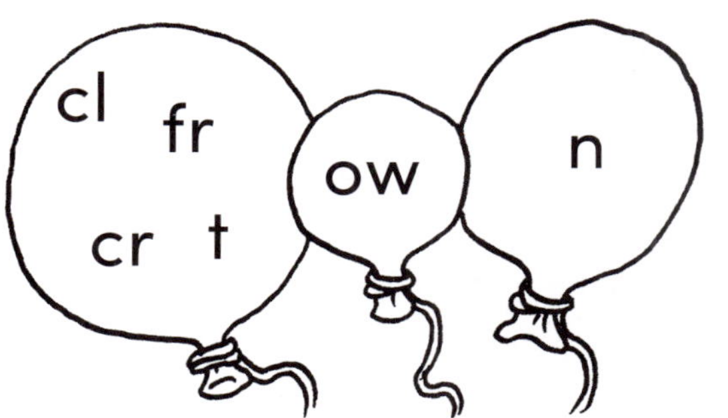

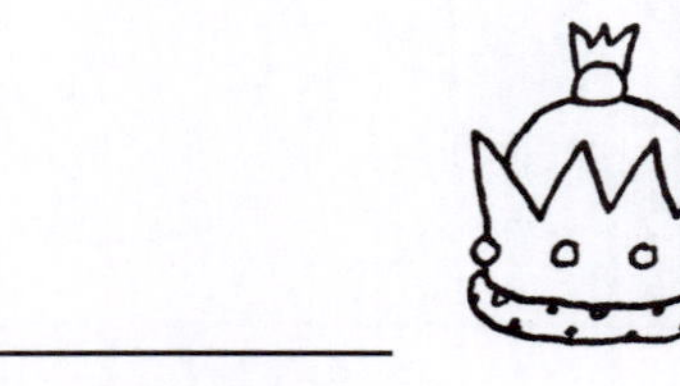

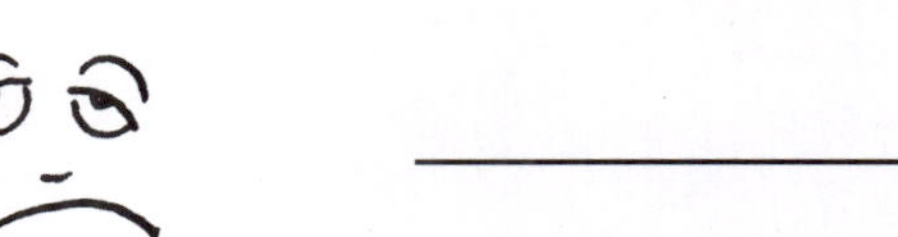

Write the words under the word that rhymes.

bow

cow

Find a small word in the list word. Write the small word.

slow ____________ grow ____________

show ____________ down ____________

Write list words.

We need to ____________ the long grass today.

My parents ____________ me to wash their car!

Use **ow** at the end of a word.

Write **ou** or **ow**.

H__ __ n__ __, br__ __n c__ __?

Go ar__ __nd to the back of the h__ __se.

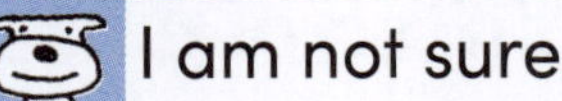

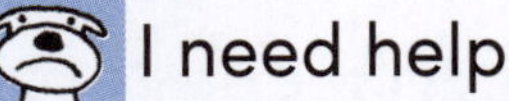

I need help.

Unit 23

My favourite sport is long jump!

Say Listen Look Understand Remember Practise	
hang	________
sang	________
king	________
bring	________
thing	________
song	________
belong	________
hung	________
sting	________
swing	________
My own words	
________	________
________	________
________	________

1 Use the clues to make list words.

 ~~d~~ → g = ________

b + = ________

 ~~i~~ → o = ________

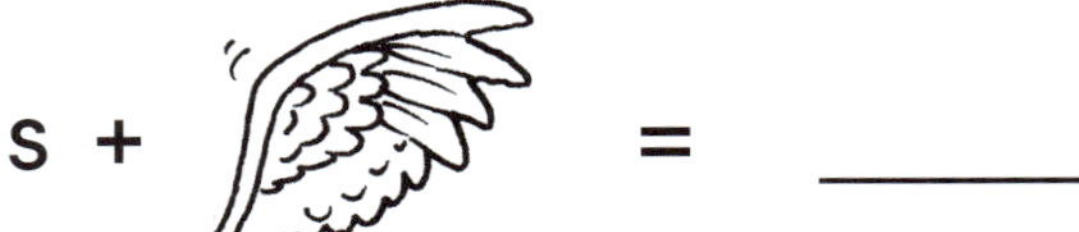

s + = ________

 ~~l~~ → t = ________

 ~~k~~ → th = ________

2 Say both words. Colour the correct one.

Monkeys like to [hung | hang] upside down.

We ran outside when the bell [rang | ring].

Mum always [sings | songs] in the car.

Spelling Rules! Student Book 1 (ISBN 9780655092674)

You can add **ing** to many words.

jump → *jumping* *look* → *looking*

Words ending in **ng** add **ing** too.

hang → *hanging* *sing* → *singing*

Add **ing** to these words.

play	______	grow	______
spell	______	go	______
sting	______	bring	______
belong	______	swing	______

Use the words in a story.

king
ring
long

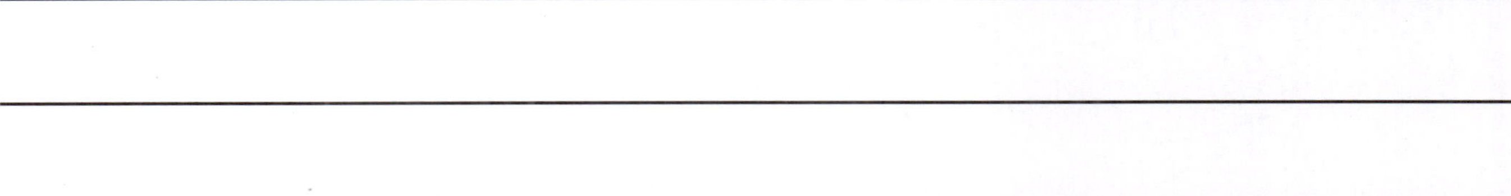

Make compound words.

some
no
any
every
thing

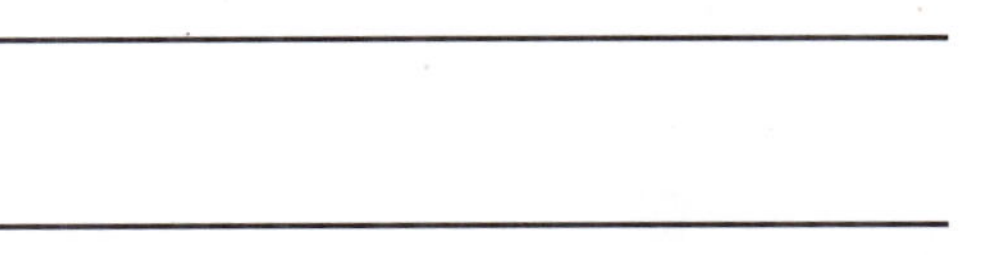

I can do this.
I am not sure.
I need help.

Unit 24 Revision

1 Say the word. Write **nt**, **nd** or **ng.**

 te__ __

 wi__ __

 wi__ __

 be__ __

 swi__ __

 pla__ __

2 Write **ou** or **ow**.

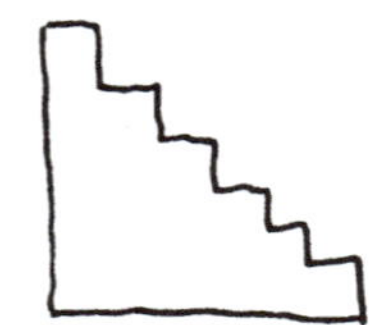 d__ __n

 m__ __th

 r__ __nd

 bl__ __

 cl__ __d

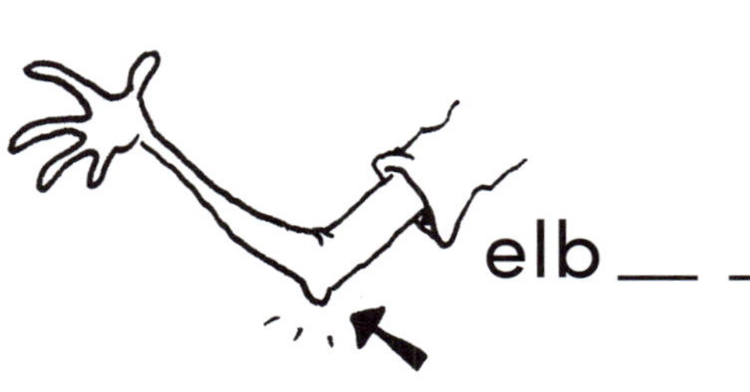 elb__ __

3 Write the first two letters.

 __ __ab

 __ __iends

__ __ag

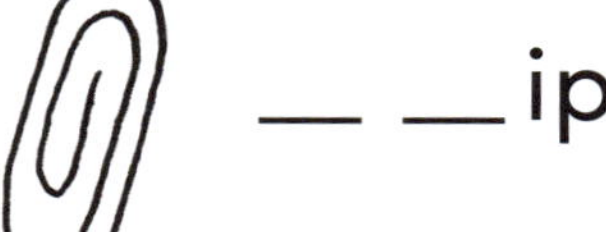 __ __ip

 __ __out

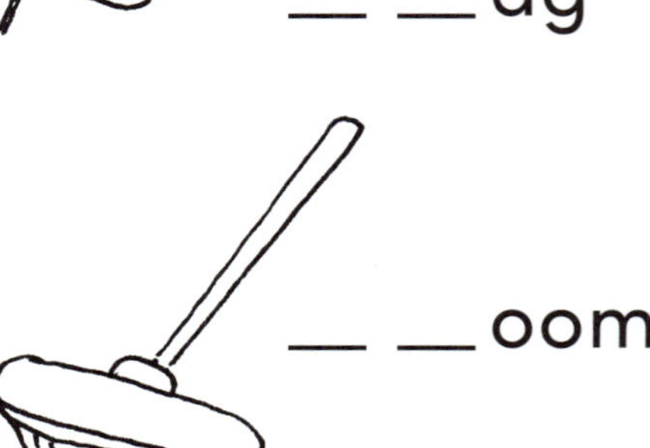 __ __oom

Spelling Rules! Student Book 1 (ISBN 9780655092674) © Janelle Ho, Helen Pearson

Finish the story. Use the words in the box.

hung	went	sang	blew

For my party Dad ________ balloons along the fence. We ________ into the garden to play hide-and-seek. Everyone ________ 'Happy Birthday'. I ________ out all the candles on my cake. Everyone cheered loudly.

Add **ed** to the words in the box. Finish the story.

show___	hunt___	shout___

Mum gave me a ring for my birthday. I ________ it to my aunt. She lost the ring. We ________ for it in the grass. Mum found it. I ________ 'Hooray!'

Find a word that means the opposite. Colour the word.

not up 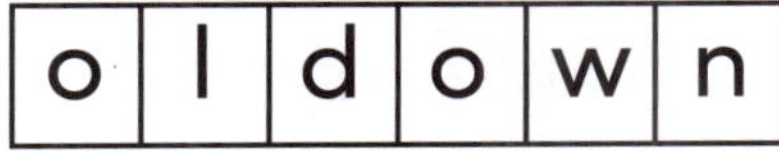

not steep 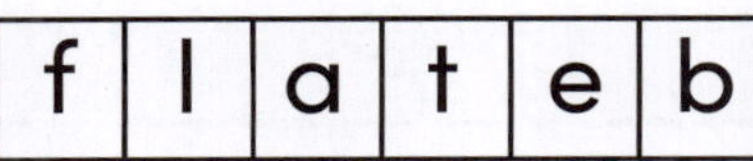

not short 

not lost 

not fast 

not quiet

p	i	l	o	u	d

Unit 25

You stink!

Thank you.

Say Listen Look Understand Remember Practise	
ink	______
pink	______
wink	______
stink	______
think	______
drink	______
bank	______
thank	______
drank	______
skunk	______
My own words	
______	______
______	______
______	______

1 Find a list word for each clue. What is the hidden word under the star?

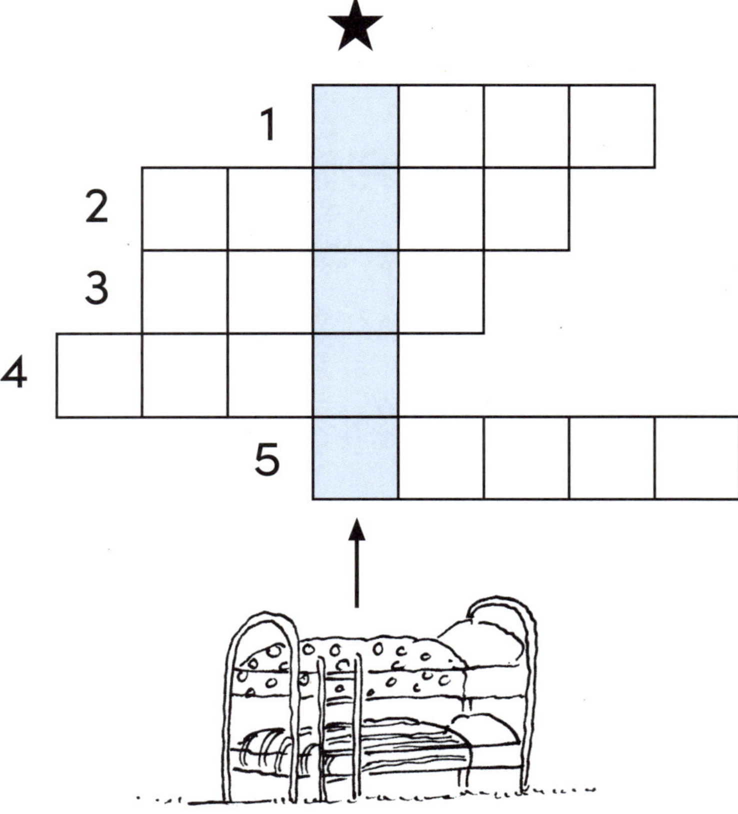

1. your money is safe here
2. animal with a bad smell
3. close one eye
4. a colour
5. a bad smell

2 Say the words. Colour the correct one.

I sent a card to | think | thank | Grandma for my present.

I dropped the soap in the bath. It | sang | sank |.

I am thirsty. May I have a | drink | drank | drunk |?

Spelling Rules! Student Book 1 (ISBN 9780655092674) © Janelle Ho, Helen Pearson

 Make words. Write the words to match the clues.

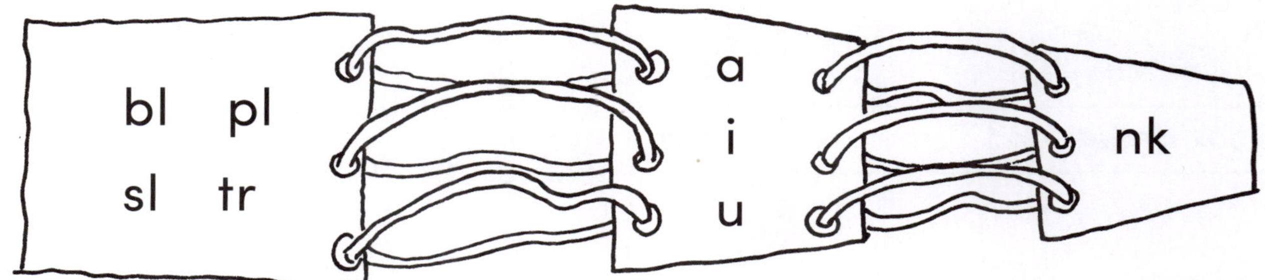

_ _ _ _ _   _ _ _ _ _   _ _ _ _ _   _ _ _ _ _

empty   piece of wood   creep   elephant's nose

4 Write the words in alphabetical order.

ink	junk	drank	think	tank

 Make a new word by adding **b**, **d**, **k** or **sh**. You can add to the beginning or end of the word or both.

rink ________   plan ________   than ________

thin ________   link ________   ran ________

 These are irregular verbs. They do not add **ed**. Follow the pattern.

ring → rang   sink → s _ nk

sing → s _ ng   drink → dr _ _ _

Reflection

I can do this.

I am not sure.

I need help.

Unit 26

I see a meal.

Say Listen Look Understand Remember Practise	
eat	________
ear	________
sea	________
meat	________
cheat	________
leaf	________
near	________
each	________
teacher	________
clean	________
My own words	
________	________
________	________
________	________

1 Write the word. Match the body part to its use.

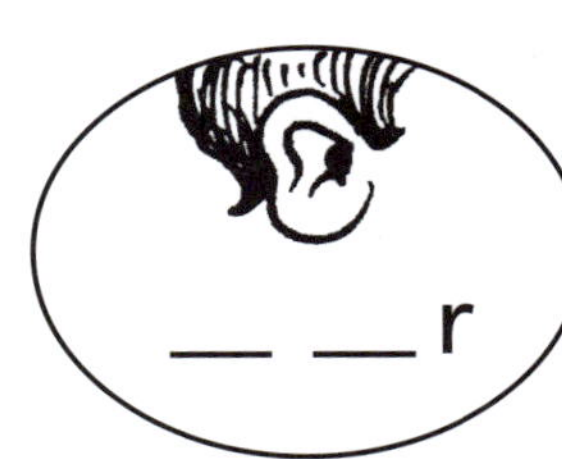

__ __r — smell

__ye — hear

n__s__ — feel

m__ __th — see

ha__ __ — taste

2 Change one letter to make a word.

clear + n	________	lean + f	________
teach + b	________	neat + m	________
fear + n	________	beak + n	________

Spelling Rules! Student Book 1 (ISBN 9780655092674) © Janelle Ho, Helen Pearson

3 Write the words.

n / f / d → ear ______ ______ ______

m / b / cl → ean ______ ______ ______

m / b / s → eat ______ ______ ______

b / t / p → each ______ ______ ______

4 Make compound words.

sea < gull ______ / shell ______

sea < weed ______ / shore ______

Tip

Some words sound the same, but are not spelt the same.

be	*sea*	*bean*	*meat*	*weak*
bee	*see*	*been*	*meet*	*week*

5 Colour the correct word.

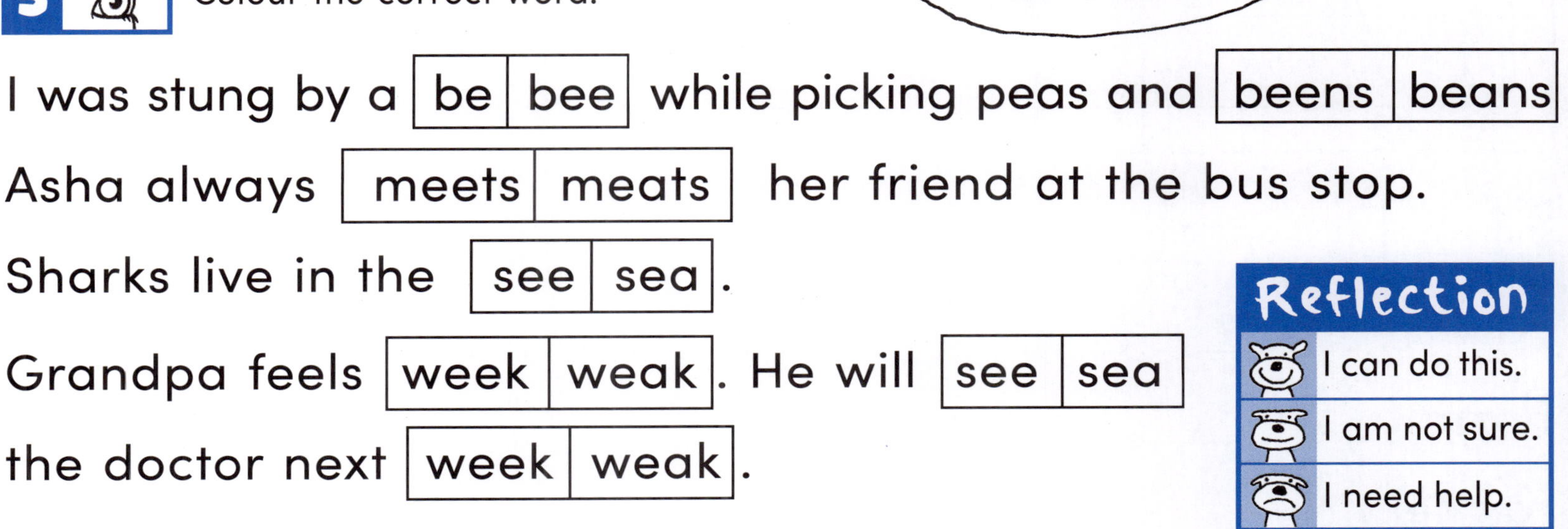

I was stung by a [be | bee] while picking peas and [beens | beans].

Asha always [meets | meats] her friend at the bus stop.

Sharks live in the [see | sea].

Grandpa feels [week | weak]. He will [see | sea] the doctor next [week | weak].

Reflection

- I can do this.
- I am not sure.
- I need help.

Unit 27

Say Listen Look Understand Remember Practise

arm	________
car	________
park	________
dark	________
star	________
start	________
hard	________
barn	________
smart	________
farmer	________
My own words	
________	________
________	________
________	________

1 Make **ar** words.

ar: c, j, b, t, f

____
____
____
____
____

ark: sh, b, m, d, p

____
____
____
____
____

2 Find a small word in the big word. Write a different small word for each.

card ________ start ________ bark ________

harm ________ barn ________ cart ________

farmer ________ heart ________ father ________

Spelling Rules! Student Book 1 (ISBN 9780655092674) © Janelle Ho, Helen Pearson

3 Finish the letter.

hard	far	farm	dark	barn	yard

Dear Uncle Carl,

I loved staying on your ________. It was so ________ at night! I liked hunting for eggs in the ________ and in the ________. It was ________ to find them in the long grass. I wish you did not live so ________ away.

Love from Mark

X X X

4 Write the **ar** word. Use both words in a sentence.

5 Circle two mistakes in each sentence.

My farther grew up on a shepe farm.

Ar these songs hart to sing?

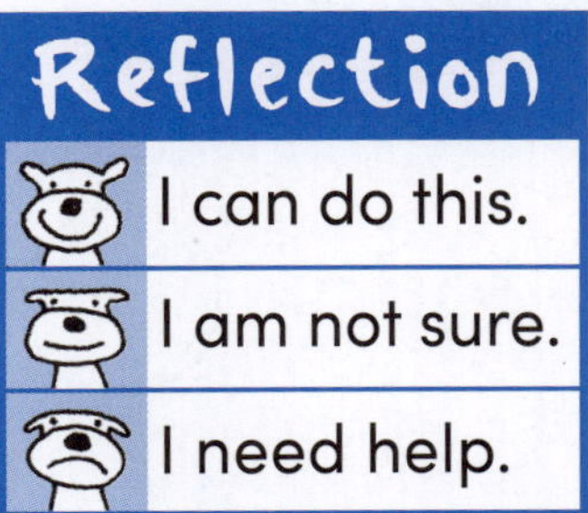

Unit 28

Don't stay away all day!

Say Listen Look Understand Remember Practise	
say	
play	
stay	
tray	
today	
away	
boy	
enjoy	
toy	
buy	
My own words	

1 Write list words.

2 A syllable makes one beat in a word.
Write the number of syllables you can hear.

today 

yesterday 

holiday 

Spelling Rules! Student Book 1 (ISBN 9780655092674) © Janelle Ho, Helen Pearson

3 Write the words. Choose one to finish the sentence.

play — s ____________ / ed ____________ / ing ____________

We __________ outside all day.

enjoy — s ____________ / ed ____________ / ing ____________

Asha __________ reading.

annoy — s ____________ / ed ____________ / ing ____________

It is ____________ to get lost.

Tip These words sound alike. *to too two* *by buy*

4 Colour the correct word.

I need | to | two | too | dollars to | by | buy | a drink.

Roy is going | to | two | too | play football today.

Do you walk to school | by | buy | yourself?

5 Write six words ending in **ay**.

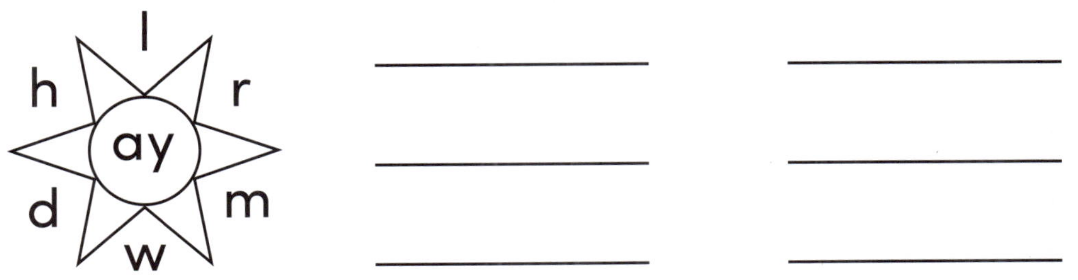

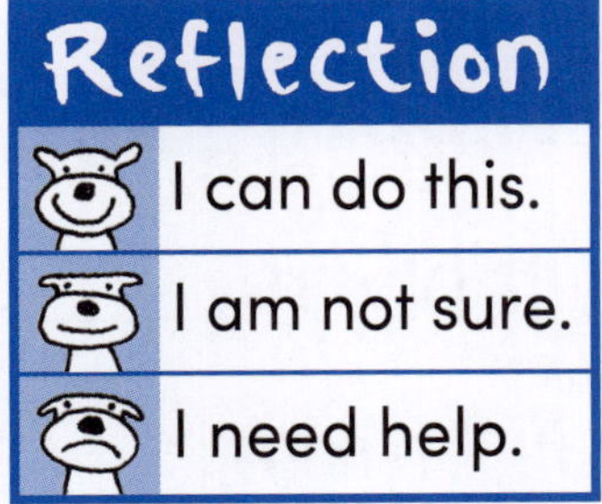

Unit 29

Say Listen Look Understand Remember Practise

bird	
girl	
stir	
dirty	
shirt	
fork	
torn	
short	
sport	
cord	
My own words	

1 Write **ir** or **or**.

c__ __d

f__ __k

c__ __k

sh__ __t

g__ __l

c__ __n

th__ __n

st__ __

2 Write a list word that rhymes.

pork	________	skirt	________
horn	________	curl	________
third	________	fur	________

Spelling Rules! Student Book 1 (ISBN 9780655092674) © Janelle Ho, Helen Pearson

3 Say both words. Colour the correct one.

I enjoy playing | sport | short | at school.

Priya fell over and tore her | short | shirt |.

No one saw Mum's feet under her long | skirt | shirt |.

4 Use the list words to write a story.

dirty
sport
torn

____

____

____

5 Make compound words. Use them in the sentences.

lady	+	bird	=	__________
girl		friend		__________
any		more		__________
bird		bath		__________

Li Na makes sure her __________ is filled with water.

There is a __________ resting on my hand.

Lori isn't Uncle Max's __________ __________.

Now she is his wife!

Reflection

- I can do this.
- I am not sure.
- I need help.

Spelling Rules! Student Book 1 (ISBN 9780655092674) © Janelle Ho, Helen Pearson

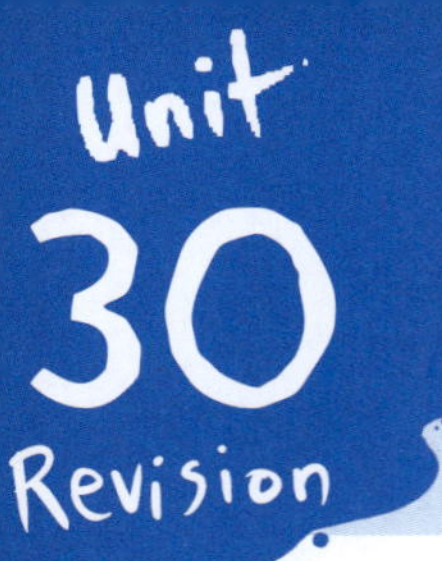

1 Write the opposite.

buy	short	start	dark	stay	hard	near	clean

soft ______________ go away ______________

end ______________ light ______________

dirty ______________ sell ______________

far ______________ tall ______________

2 Write a rhyming word with the same letter pattern.

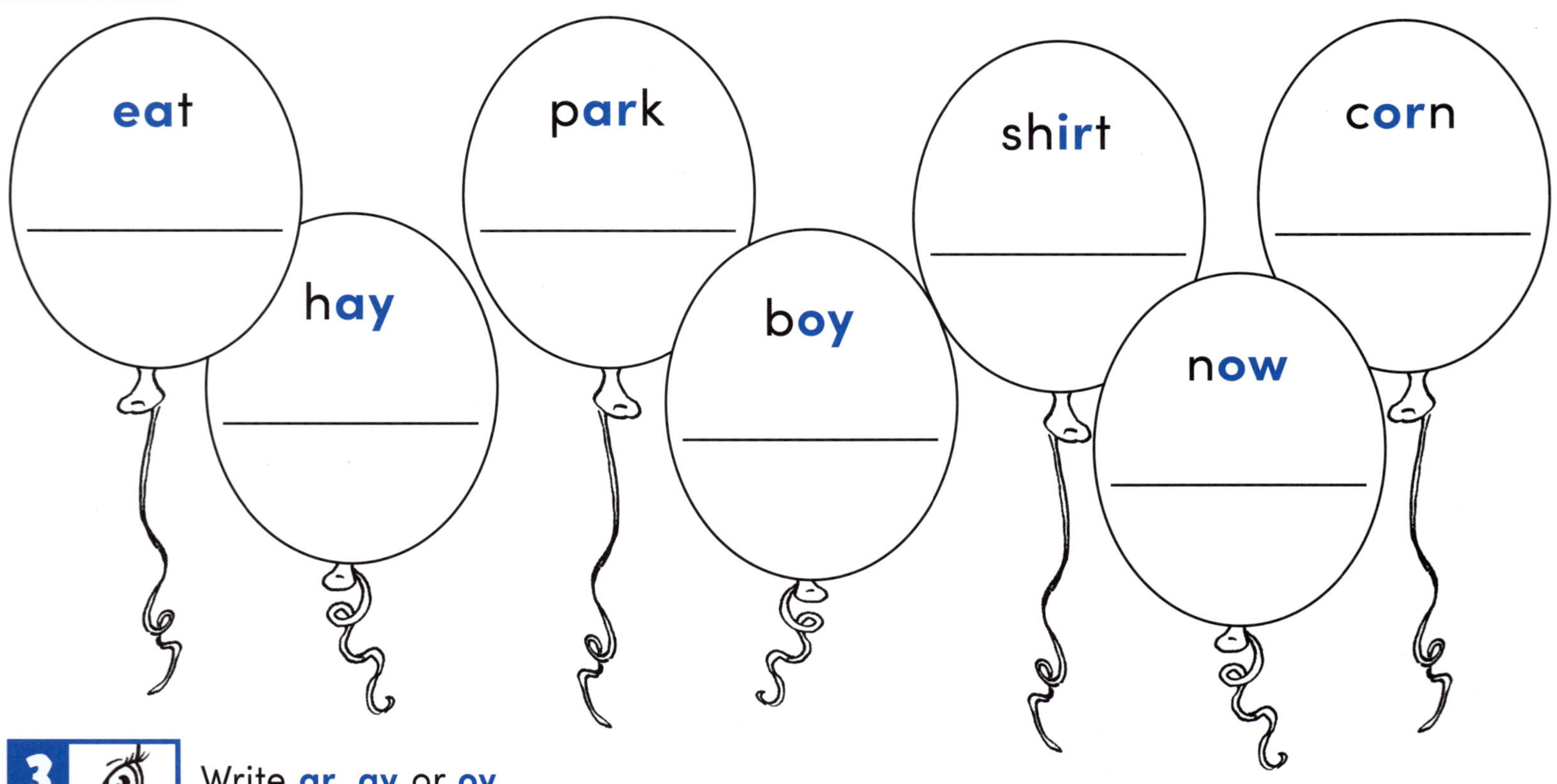

3 Write **ar**, **ay** or **oy**.

Do you enj__ __ pl__ __ing c__ __d games?

Mum was ann__ __ed when she lost her sm__ __t watch.

Usha st__ __ts her homework with the h__ __dest task.

Spelling Rules! Student Book 1 (ISBN 9780655092674) © Janelle Ho, Helen Pearson

4 It is dark in the barn. Name the animals.

_ _ _   _ _ _ _ _   _ _ _ _   _ _ _   _ _ _ _ _

5 Write **or**, **ee**, **ea**, or **ir**.

l_ _f   f_ _k   str_ _t   sk_ _t

6 Write **nd**, **nt**, **ng** or **nk**.

wi_ _   wi_ _   ki_ _   te_ _

7 Write a word to match each clue. Draw a picture of the hidden word.

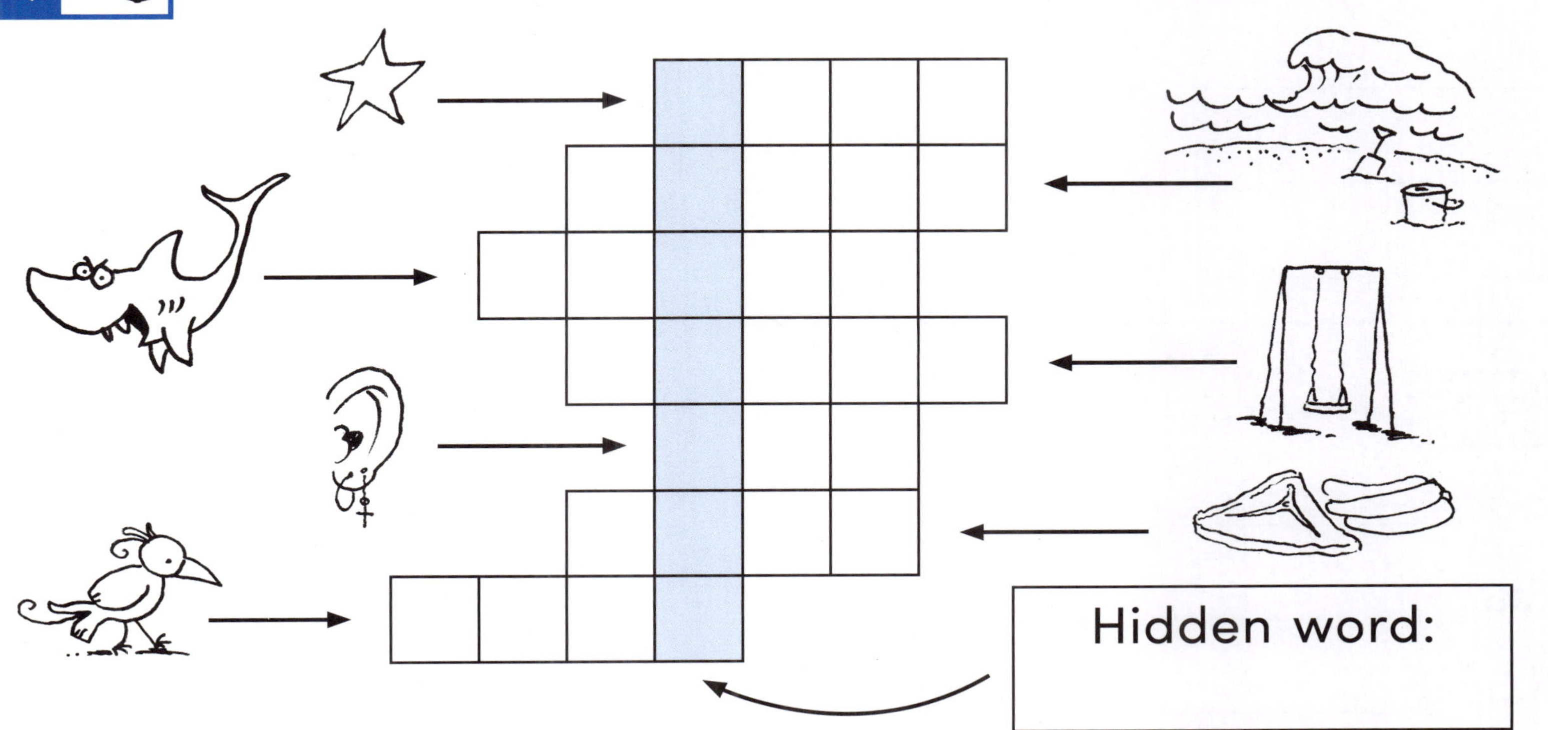

Unit 31

Say Listen Look Understand Remember Practise	
one	___
two	___
three	___
four	___
five	___
six	___
seven	___
eight	___
nine	___
ten	___
My own words	
___	___
___	___
___	___

1 Write the number and the plural word. Remember not all plural words have **s**.

___ ___

___ ___

___ ___

___ ___

___ ___

2 Write the number that rhymes. Remember that the spelling may be different!

door	___	free	___	bun	___
ticks	___	gate	___	men	___
shoe	___	hive	___	line	___

3 Write the numbers.

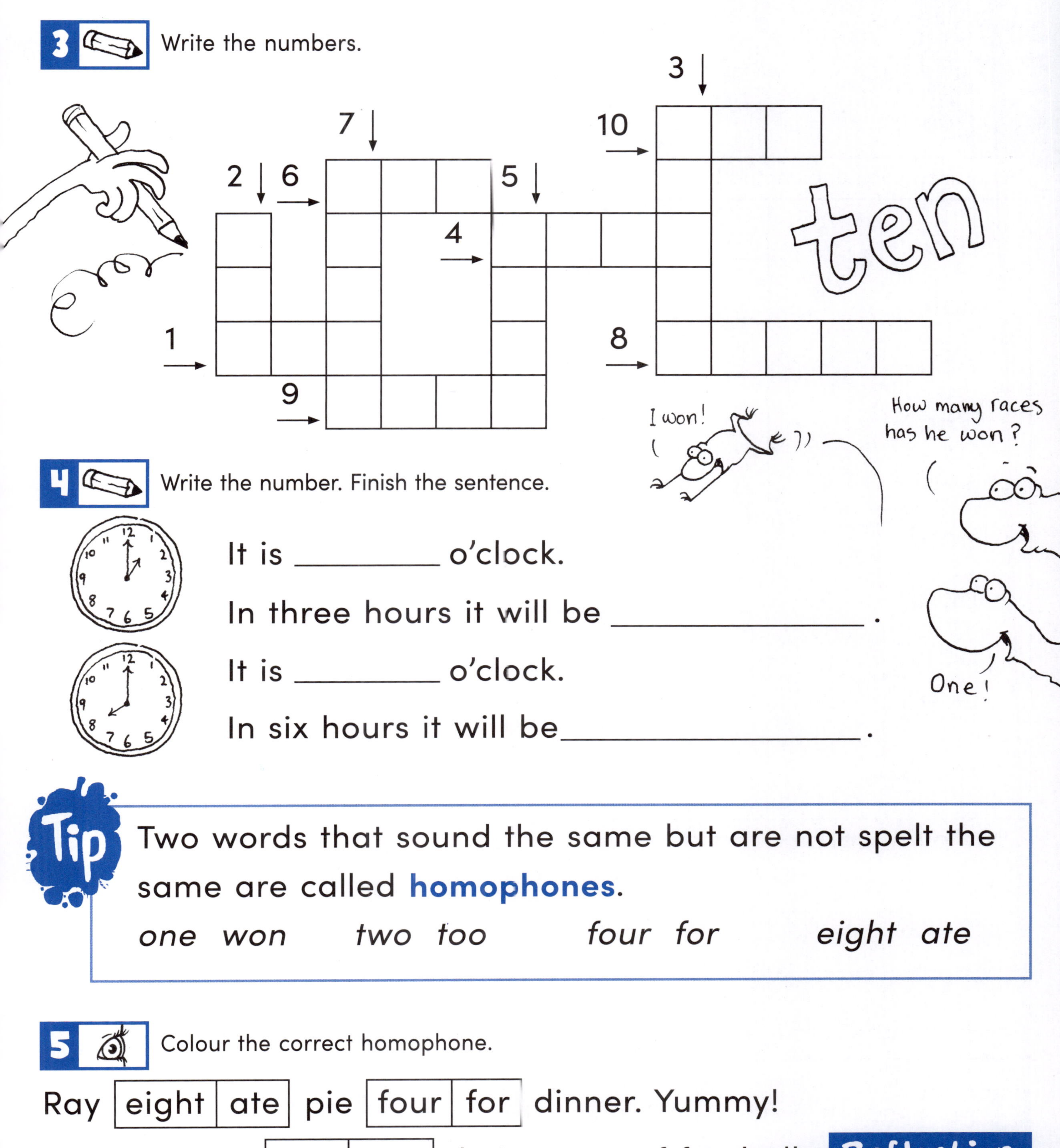

4 Write the number. Finish the sentence.

It is __________ o'clock.

In three hours it will be __________________.

It is __________ o'clock.

In six hours it will be __________________.

Tip Two words that sound the same but are not spelt the same are called **homophones**.

one won *two too* *four for* *eight ate*

5 Colour the correct homophone.

Ray | eight | ate | pie | four | for | dinner. Yummy!

Maya's team | one | won | their game of football.

Mandeep's team won | two | too | !

I have | two | too | cats and | one | won | dog.

Reflection

- I can do this.
- I am not sure.
- I need help.

Unit 32

You are almost old enough to jump!

Say Listen Look Understand Remember Practise	
old	________
cold	________
gold	________
told	________
sold	________
hold	________
held	________
bald	________
build	________
world	________
My own words	
________	________
________	________
________	________

1 Write six old words.

f, g, h, c, t, b — old

________ ________
________ ________
________ ________

2 Take out the l. Write the new word.

bald ________
world ________

3 Say both words. Colour the correct one.

A [bald | bold] man has no hair.

Can you [held | hold] my bag, please?

This is the house that Jack [build | built].

Spelling Rules! Student Book 1 (ISBN 9780655092674) © Janelle Ho, Helen Pearson

Tip Some words have letters you cannot hear.

often *listen*

castle *whistle*

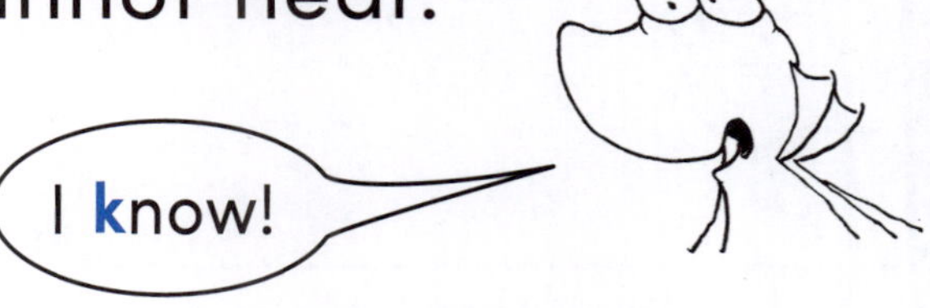

4 Write a sentence using both words.

build castle	____________________ ____________________

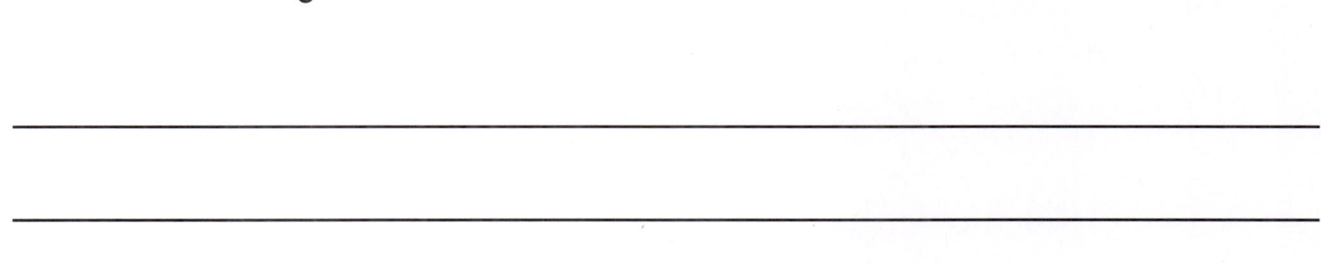

listen whistle	____________________ ____________________

5 Write the past tense for these irregular verbs.

tell __________ sell __________

hold __________ build __________

Rule Add **er** to compare two things.

tall → taller *fast → faster*

6 Colour the correct word.

The room was | dark | darker | after Dad turned off the light.

I will buy a | small | smaller | gift for my teacher.

My sister is | old | older | than my brother but she is | short | shorter | than him.

Lula loves the | green | greener | grass in spring.

Unit 33

I can't wait to see you hop!

Say Listen Look Understand Remember Practise	
air	
hair	
chair	
stair	
tail	
sail	
snail	
train	
wait	
said	
My own words	

1 Make ai words.

t r s n j ail

h f ch p st air

2 Write the word. Find a small word inside the word.

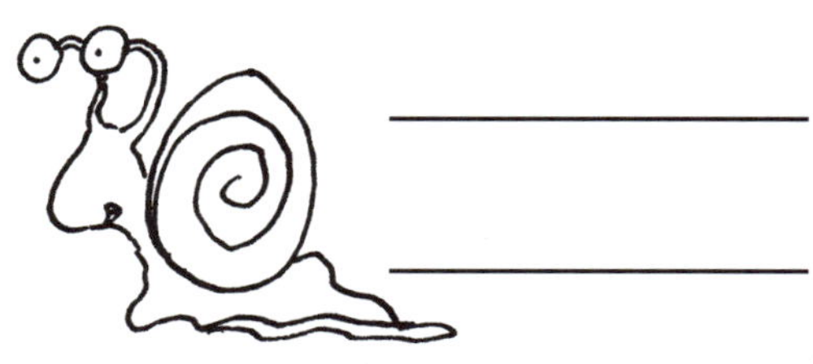

Spelling Rules! Student Book 1 (ISBN 9780655092674) © Janelle Ho, Helen Pearson

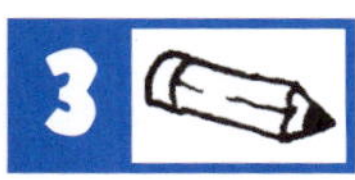 Make compound words. Use each word in a sentence.

 + coat

____

____

finger + 

____

____

 + brush

____

____

4 The three little pigs have built new houses. What did they use? Fill in the missing letters and add **said**.

Pig 1 = 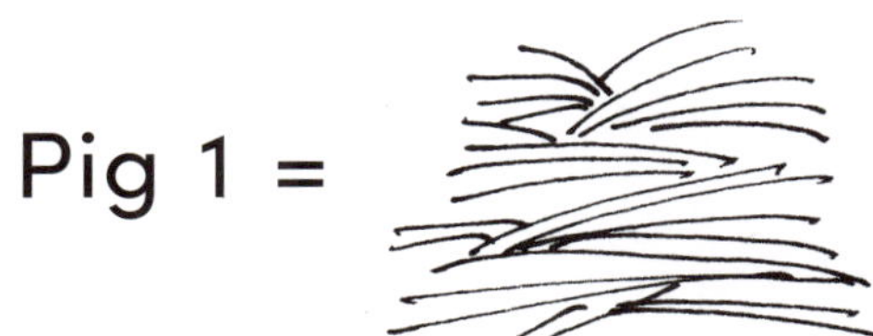 Pig 2 =  Pig 3 = 

'I built my house out of __traw,' _______ the first pig.

'I built my house out of w__ __d,' _______ the second pig.

'I built my house out of br__ __ __s,' _______ the third pig.

 Colour the correct homophone.

Take care not to trip on the | stare | stair |.

Don't | stare | stair | out the window! 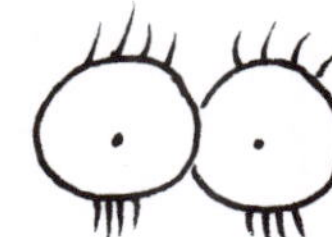

This car is for | sail | sale |.

Let's | sail | sale | to the island.

Reflection

- I can do this.
- I am not sure.
- I need help.

Unit 34

Say Listen Look Understand Remember Practise	
who	___
why	___
when	___
where	___
what	___
which	___
whose	___
wheel	___
white	___
wheat	___
My own words	
___	___
___	___
___	___

1 Find small words in the list word. Write the small words.

when ___ ___

what ___ ___

wheel ___ ___

white ___ ___

wheat ___ ___ ___

where ___ ___ ___

2 Write the words.

w — ipe ___
w — eak ___
w — all ___

wh — eel ___
wh — ite ___
wh — ale ___

3 Choose the correct word for each riddle.

why	where	what	when	which

_ _ _ did the boy take a ruler to bed?

To see how long he slept.

_ _ _ _ can a net hold water?

When the water is ice.

_ _ _ _ can run but not walk?

Your nose.

_ _ _ _ _ do frogs keep their money?

In river banks.

_ _ _ _ _ pet only lives on the floor?

A carpet.

Ha ha ha ha ha ha

4 Write a list word that rhymes. Remember to listen to the sound.

two	pie	zoos	mare
________	________	________	________

5 Write your own question and answer.

Question: Wh ____________________________

____

Answer: ________________________________

____

Reflection

- I can do this.
- I am not sure.
- I need help.

Unit 35 Revision

Hop with the frog from leaf to leaf.

START

1 Good lu__ __!

2 b__ __ __

9 c__k__

10 sm__l__

11 __ __ips

13 de__ __

14 __ __a__ __

21 __ __ie__ __s

22 d__ __n

23 __i__ __

25 sk__ __ __

26 l__ __f

33 ch__ __ __

34 __ __y

THE END!

Spelling Rules! Student Book 1 (ISBN 9780655092674) © Janelle Ho, Helen Pearson

Fill in the missing letters to match each picture.
If you need help, the number tells you which unit to look at.

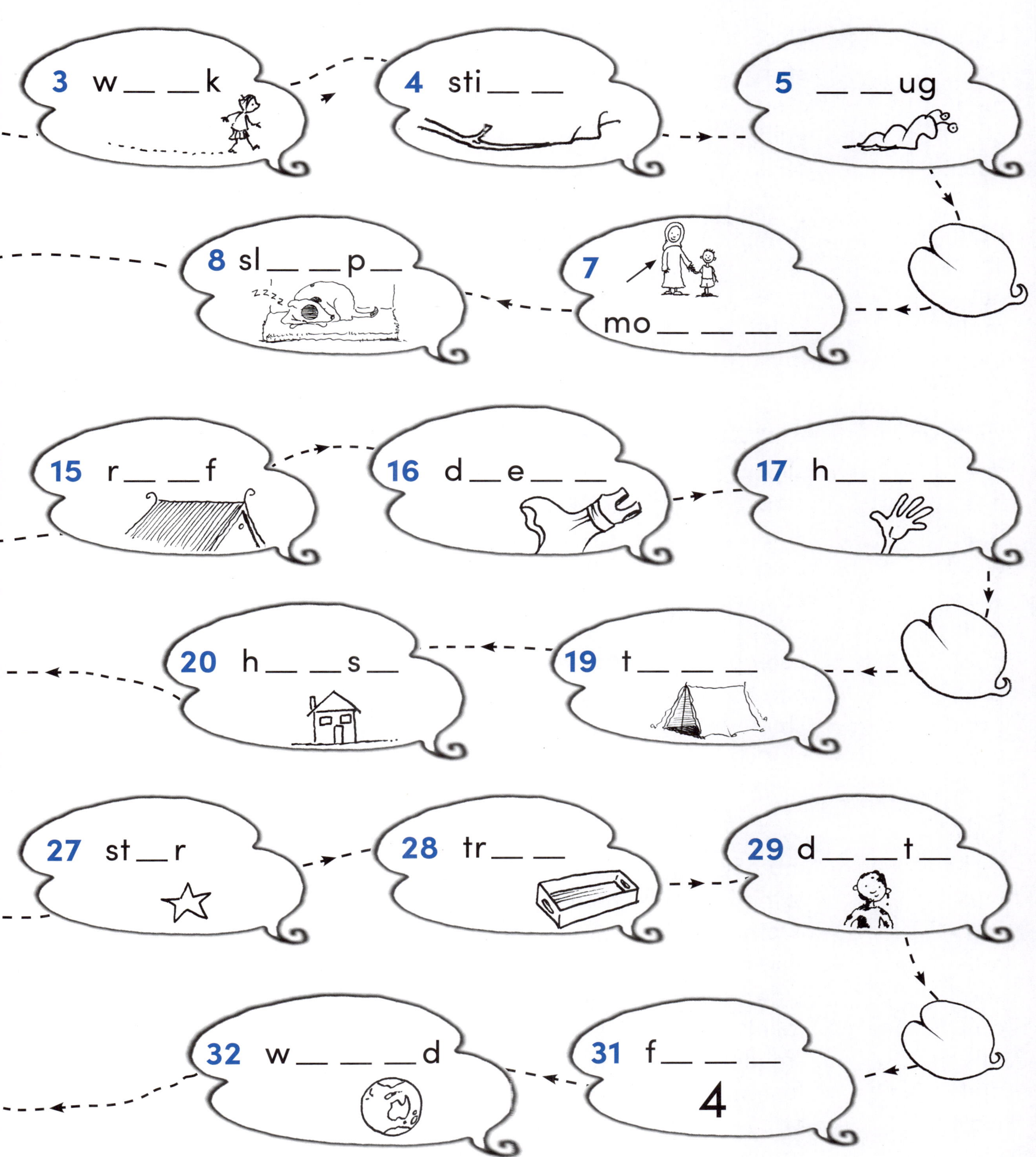

List words in unit order

Unit 1
rip
dish
quit
quick
ban
than
shack
let
moth
luck

Unit 2
see
bee
feet
week
sheep
look
book
foot
good
wool

Unit 3
all
wall
fall
fell
shall
dull
full
pull
walk
talk

Unit 4
stop
step
still
stick
rest
fast
list
lost
must
last

Unit 5
slip
slop
slap
slug
slid
sly
asleep
small
smell
smash

Unit 7
mother
father
brother
sister
elder
taller
smaller
faster
baby
family

Unit 8
jelly
silly
hilly
happy
pretty
sunny
hurry
sleepy
hobby
body

Unit 9
ate
cake
take
late
date
name
awake
here
eve
these

Unit 10
like
hide
smile
fine
toe
nose
hope
stone
rude
ruler

Unit 11
chop
chat
chips
check
child
children
chase
rich
much
such

Unit 13
spine
speech
snap
snore
snack
skin
skate
wasp
ask
desk

Unit 14
fly
flag
flash
clap
club
clock
plant
place
blast
blue

Unit 15
zoo
pool
room
moon
roof
tooth
food
spoon
school
balloon

Unit 16
kiss
mess
fuss
class
dress
plus
minus
cents
recess
buzz

Unit 17
end
send
sand
kind
wind
pond
stand
handshake
grandmother
grandfather

Spelling Rules! Student Book 1 (ISBN 9780655092674) © Janelle Ho, Helen Pearson

Unit 19
tree
crab
frog
from
pram
drive
grape
green
broom
friend

Unit 20
ant
want
went
sent
spent
bent
front
hunt
aunt
uncle

Unit 21
our
loud
cloud
house
mouse
shout
mouth
found
around
about

Unit 22
owl
mow
how
slow
show
grow
down
brown
allow
yellow

Unit 23
hang
sang
king
bring
thing
song
belong
hung
sting
swing

Unit 25
ink
pink
wink
stink
think
drink
bank
thank
drank
skunk

Unit 26
eat
ear
sea
meat
cheat
leaf
near
each
teacher
clean

Unit 27
arm
car
park
dark
star
start
hard
barn
smart
farmer

Unit 28
say
play
stay
tray
today
away
boy
enjoy
toy
buy

Unit 29
bird
girl
stir
dirty
shirt
fork
torn
short
sport
cord

Unit 31
one
two
three
four
five
six
seven
eight
nine
ten

Unit 32
old
cold
gold
told
sold
hold
held
bald
build
world

Unit 33
air
hair
chair
stair
tail
sail
snail
train
wait
said

Unit 34
who
why
when
where
what
which
whose
wheel
white
wheat

List words in alphabetical order

about	Unit 21
air	Unit 33
all	Unit 3
allow	Unit 22
ant	Unit 20
arm	Unit 27
around	Unit 21
ask	Unit 13
asleep	Unit 5
ate	Unit 9
aunt	Unit 20
awake	Unit 9
away	Unit 28
baby	Unit 7
bald	Unit 32
balloon	Unit 15
ban	Unit 1
bank	Unit 25
barn	Unit 27
bee	Unit 2
belong	Unit 23
bent	Unit 20
bird	Unit 29
blast	Unit 14
blue	Unit 14
body	Unit 8
book	Unit 2
boy	Unit 28
bring	Unit 23
broom	Unit 19
brother	Unit 7
brown	Unit 22
build	Unit 32
buy	Unit 28
buzz	Unit 16
cake	Unit 9
car	Unit 27
cents	Unit 16
chair	Unit 33
chase	Unit 11
chat	Unit 11
cheat	Unit 26
check	Unit 11
child	Unit 11
children	Unit 11
chips	Unit 11
chop	Unit 11
clap	Unit 14
class	Unit 16
clean	Unit 26
clock	Unit 14
cloud	Unit 21
club	Unit 14
cold	Unit 32
cord	Unit 29
crab	Unit 19
dark	Unit 27
date	Unit 9
desk	Unit 13
dirty	Unit 29
dish	Unit 1
down	Unit 22
drank	Unit 25
dress	Unit 16
drink	Unit 25
drive	Unit 19
dull	Unit 3
each	Unit 26
ear	Unit 26
eat	Unit 26
eight	Unit 31
elder	Unit 7
end	Unit 17
eve	Unit 9
fall	Unit 3
family	Unit 7
farmer	Unit 27
fast	Unit4
faster	Unit 7
father	Unit 7
feet	Unit 2
fell	Unit 3
fine	Unit 10
five	Unit 31
flag	Unit 14
flash	Unit 14
fly	Unit 14
food	Unit 15
foot	Unit 2
fork	Unit 29
found	Unit 21
four	Unit 31
friend	Unit 19
frog	Unit 19
from	Unit 19
front	Unit 20
full	Unit 3
fuss	Unit 16
girl	Unit 29
gold	Unit 32
good	Unit 2
grandfather	Unit 17
grandmother	Unit 17
grape	Unit 19
green	Unit 19
grow	Unit 22
hair	Unit 33
handshake	Unit 17
hang	Unit 23
happy	Unit 8
hard	Unit 27
held	Unit 32
here	Unit 9
hide	Unit 10
hilly	Unit 8
hobby	Unit 8
hold	Unit 32
hope	Unit 10
house	Unit 21
how	Unit 22
hung	Unit 23
hunt	Unit 20
hurry	Unit 8
ink	Unit 25
jelly	Unit 8
joy	Unit 28
kind	Unit 17
king	Unit 23
kiss	Unit 16
last	Unit4
late	Unit 9
leaf	Unit 26
let	Unit 1
like	Unit 10
list	Unit4
look	Unit 2
lost	Unit4
loud	Unit 21
luck	Unit 1
meat	Unit 26
mess	Unit 16
minus	Unit 16
moon	Unit 15
moth	Unit 1
mother	Unit 7
mouse	Unit 21
mouth	Unit 21
mow	Unit 22
much	Unit 11
must	Unit4

Spelling Rules! Student Book 1 (ISBN 9780655092674) © Janelle Ho, Helen Pearson

name	Unit 9
near	Unit 26
nine	Unit 31
nose	Unit 10
old	Unit 32
one	Unit 31
our	Unit 21
owl	Unit 22
park	Unit 27
pink	Unit 25
place	Unit 14
plant	Unit 14
play	Unit 28
plus	Unit 16
pond	Unit 17
pool	Unit 15
pram	Unit 19
pretty	Unit 8
pull	Unit 3
quick	Unit 1
quit	Unit 1
recess	Unit 16
rest	Unit4
rich	Unit 11
rip	Unit 1
roof	Unit 15
room	Unit 15
rude	Unit 10
ruler	Unit 10
said	Unit 33
sail	Unit 33
sand	Unit 17
sang	Unit 23
say	Unit 28
school	Unit 15
sea	Unit 26
see	Unit 2
send	Unit 17
sent	Unit 20
seven	Unit 31
shack	Unit 1
shall	Unit 3
sheep	Unit 2
shirt	Unit 29
short	Unit 29
shout	Unit 21
show	Unit 22
silly	Unit 8
sister	Unit 7
six	Unit 31
skate	Unit 13
skin	Unit 13
skunk	Unit 25
slap	Unit 5
sleepy	Unit 8
slid	Unit 5
slip	Unit 5
slop	Unit 5
slow	Unit 22
slug	Unit 5
sly	Unit 5
small	Unit 5
smaller	Unit 7
smart	Unit 27
smash	Unit 5
smell	Unit 5
smile	Unit 10
snack	Unit 13
snail	Unit 33
snap	Unit 13
snore	Unit 13
sold	Unit 32
song	Unit 23
speech	Unit 13
spent	Unit 20
spine	Unit 13
spoon	Unit 15
sport	Unit 29
stair	Unit 33
stand	Unit 17
star	Unit 27
start	Unit 27
stay	Unit 28
step	Unit4
stick	Unit4
still	Unit4
sting	Unit 23
stink	Unit 25
stir	Unit 29
stone	Unit 10
stop	Unit4
such	Unit 11
sunny	Unit 8
swing	Unit 23
tail	Unit 33
take	Unit 9
talk	Unit 3
taller	Unit 7
teacher	Unit 26
ten	Unit 31
than	Unit 1
thank	Unit 25
these	Unit 9
thing	Unit 23
think	Unit 25
three	Unit 31
today	Unit 28
toe	Unit 10
told	Unit 32
torn	Unit 29
toy	Unit 28
tooth	Unit 15
train	Unit 33
tray	Unit 28
tree	Unit 19
two	Unit 31
uncle	Unit 20
wait	Unit 33
walk	Unit 3
wall	Unit 3
want	Unit 20
wasp	Unit 13
week	Unit 2
went	Unit 20
what	Unit 34
wheat	Unit 34
wheel	Unit 34
when	Unit 34
where	Unit 34
which	Unit 34
white	Unit 34
who	Unit 34
whose	Unit 34
why	Unit 34
wind	Unit 17
wink	Unit 25
wool	Unit 2
world	Unit 32
yellow	Unit 22
zoo	Unit 15

SPELLING RULES AND TIPS

- Most words add **s** to show there is more than one. *chip* → *chips*
  Some words change. *man* → *men*   *child* → *children*
  Some words stay the same. *sheep*   *deer*   *fish*

- You can add **y** to some words to make an adjective.
  sleep → *sleepy*

- Most words add **ed** to show an action happened in the past.
  pack → *packed*
  Some words change. They are called **irregular verbs**.
  is → *was*   *send* → *sent*   *ring* → *rang*

- You can add **ing** to many words.
  jump → *jumping*   *look* → *looking*
  Words ending in **ng** add **ing** too.
  hang → *hanging*   *sing* → *singing*

- You can add **er** to compare two things.
  all → *taller*   *fast* → *faster*

- Two words that are joined together to make a new word is called a **compound word**. *sun* + *hat* → *sunhat*

- Words that sound the same but are not spelt the same are called **homophones**.
  see/sea   *one/won*   *two/too*   *four/for*   *stare/stair*

- Some words have letters you cannot hear. *often*   *listen*

- **ss** and **zz** do not start a word.

- Use **a** before a consonant. *a frog*
  Use **an** before a vowel. *an owl*

Spelling Rules! Student Book 1 (ISBN 9780655092674) © Janelle Ho, Helen Pearson